GW00367411

THE BRIDGESTONE
100 BEST RESTAURANTS IN IRELAND 2006

THE BRIDGESTONE

100 BEST
RESTAURANTS
IN IRELAND 2006

JOHN McKENNA - SALLY McKENNA

ESTRAGON PRESS

FIRST PUBLISHED IN 2005

BY ESTRAGON PRESS

DURRUS

COUNTY CORK

© ESTRAGON PRESS

TEXT © JOHN & SALLY McKENNA

THE MORAL RIGHT OF THE AUTHORS HAS

BEEN ASSERTED

ISBN 1 87407670 7

PRINTED IN SPAIN BY GRAPHYCEMS

WRITTEN BY JOHN McKENNA

CONTRIBUTING EDITORS:

EAMON BARRETT

ORLA BRODERICK

ELIZABETH FIELD

CLAIRE GOODWILLIE

LESLIE WILLIAMS

CAROLINE WORKMAN

PUBLISHING EDITOR: SALLY McKENNA

EDITOR: JUDITH CASEY

N. I. CONTRIBUTOR: HARRY OWENS

ART DIRECTION BY NICK CANN

COVER PHOTOS BY MIKE O'TOOLE

ILLUSTRATIONS BY AOIFE WASSER

WEB: FLUIDEDGE.IE

FOR:

Sean Buckley

WITH THANKS TO
Des Collins, Colm Conyngham, Pat Curran,
Julie Barrett, John & Gill Bensley, Josette Cadoret,
Nick Cann, Frieda Forde,
George Lane, Frank McKevitt, Mike O'Toole,
Miguel Sancho, Hugh Stancliffe,
Ann Marie Tobin, Lorraine Ward.

We greatly appreciate receiving reports, e-mails and
criticisms from readers, and would like to thank those
who have written in the past, whose opinions are of
enormous assistance to us when considering which 100
restaurants finally make it into this book.

Bridgestone is the world's largest tyre and rubber company

• Founded in Japan in 1931, it currently employs over 100,000 people in Europe, Asia and America and its products are sold in more than 150 countries. Its European plants are situated in France, Spain, Italy, Poland and Turkey.

• Bridgestone manufacture tyres for a wide variety of vehicles from passenger cars and motorcycles, trucks and buses to giant earthmovers and aircraft.

• Many new cars are fitted with Bridgestone tyres during manufacture, including Ford, Toyota, Volkswagen, Mercedes and BMW. Ferrari and Porsche are also fitted with Bridgestone performance tyres as original equipment.

• Bridgestone commercial vehicle tyres enjoy a worldwide reputation for durability and its aircraft tyres are used by more than 100 airlines.

• In Formula 1 Bridgestone supply tyres to leading teams and drivers, including Ferrari and Michael Schumacher. Technology developed in the sport has led to increased performance and safety in Bridgestone's road tyres.

BRIDGESTONE TYRES

• Bridgestone tyres are distributed in Ireland by Bridgestone Ireland Ltd, a subsidiary of the multinational Bridgestone Corporation. A wide range of tyres is stocked in its 70,000 square foot central warehouse and its staff provide sales, technical and delivery services all over Ireland.

• Bridgestone tyres are available from First Stop Tyre Centres and tyre dealers throughout Ireland.

FOR FURTHER INFORMATION:

BRIDGESTONE IRELAND LTD
10 Fingal Bay Business Park
Balbriggan
County Dublin

Tel: + 353 1 841 0000
Fax: + 353 1 841 5245

websites:
www.bridgestone-eu.com
www.firststop-eu.com

• This is the 15th edition of the Bridgestone 100 Best Guides, and this new edition comes at the end of a year when the Irish nation has been obsessing about value for money in Irish restaurants.

• Well, there are restaurants in here where you can buy a dish for one euro, and places where a menu will cost you one hundred and ten euro. Where is the value? Simple: value lies in paying money for real food cooked by creative people, and you will often find these people in the most simple of places. You don't get value when you get what we call facsimile food, served in grand rooms where menus read well, and then eat badly, because they are trapped in pretentiousness, or some crazy idea called "fine dining" a concept, which as far as we can see, is just petit-bourgeois snobbery.

• You discover value when you discover the work of talented people who are passionate about what they do, and who do it in an original way. Never mind the trappings: just feel the quality.

• Trying to find those people has been the mission of the Bridgestone 100 Best Guides since 1992. And this year, as in every year, we have found that the best cooking in Ireland is always also the best value for money.

John & Sally McKenna
Durrus, West Cork, October 2005

'If you speak the language of restaurants, you can get what you want: better service, better food, reservations and overall experience... I firmly believe that if you love restaurants for the right reasons, they will love you back.'

– Steven A. Shaw, *Turning the Tables: Restaurants from the inside out* **Harper Collins 2005.**

• Steven Shaw's book on his life and work as a writer about American restaurants is full of audacious quotes like the two above, expressions that a European sensibility initially denounces as bunkum.

• After all, it is not for the customer to speak the language of the restaurant, it is for the restaurant to speak the language of the customer, right? And whilst we will love our favourite restaurants for personal reasons, we are not under an obligation to love them, just so that they will love us back. Do we want them to love us back? Surely not. We just want them to do their job well. The love relationship in a restaurant, after all, is supposed to be with the person sitting across the table from you, face illuminated by candlelight.

**on top of
their game**

a classic

new!

• But Mr Shaw does have a point, albeit that it isn't quite the point he wants to make. It is useful to know the language of restaurants, but to use it to hustle a better table is not the correct thing to do. Knowing how restaurants work allows you to be more comfortable and confident in a restaurant. What we have learnt over many years is that people whose confidence evaporates when they walk into a restaurant, folk who are terrified of a wine list, are people who never enjoy the experience. They order and drink the same thing every time.

• A little food and wine knowledge is a wonderful thing, because it will help you get the best out of the most marvellous theatrical experience in the world: eating in a restaurant. Restaurants don't want you to love them. What they want is that all the effort, all the toil and striving, should win your appreciation. A good customer is a restaurant's admirer, not its paramour.

on top of their game

Alden's, Belfast
Avoca, Kilmacanogue
Ballymaloe House, Shanagarry
The Ballymore Inn, Ballymore Eustace
Brocka-on-the-Water, Kilgarvan
Café Paradiso, Cork
Cherry Tree Restaurant, Killaloe
Chez Hans, Cashel
Chapter One, Dublin
Coast Townhouse, Tramore
Dim Sum, Belfast
L'Ecrivain, Dublin
Good Things Café, Durrus
Jacob's on the Mall, Cork
James Street South, Belfast
Kinsale Gourmet Store, Kinsale
Longueville House, Mallow
MacNean Bistro, Cavan
La Marine, Rosslare
Mermaid Café, Dublin
Mill Restaurant, Dunfanaghy
Mint, Dublin
Nick's Warehouse, Belfast
The Nuremore Hotel, Carrickmacross
O'Connell's, Dublin
Otto's Creative Catering, Dunworley
Richmond House, Cappoquin
The Tannery, Dungarvan
Thornton's, Dublin

a classic

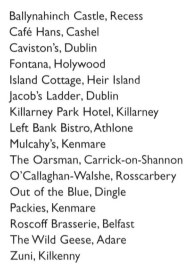

Ballynahinch Castle, Recess
Café Hans, Cashel
Caviston's, Dublin
Fontana, Holywood
Island Cottage, Heir Island
Jacob's Ladder, Dublin
Killarney Park Hotel, Killarney
Left Bank Bistro, Athlone
Mulcahy's, Kenmare
The Oarsman, Carrick-on-Shannon
O'Callaghan-Walshe, Rosscarbery
Out of the Blue, Dingle
Packies, Kenmare
Roscoff Brasserie, Belfast
The Wild Geese, Adare
Zuni, Kilkenny

new entries and re-entries for 2005

Aroma, Donegal
China House, Dublin
Crocket's on the Quay, Ballina
Eden, Dublin
Ferndale, Enniskillen
L'Gueleton, Dublin
Ginger, Belfast
Grangecon, Blessington
Lily Mai's, Golden
Macau, Belfast
Mackerel, Dublin
Mossie's, Adrigole
Rathmullan House, Rathmullan
Shu, Belfast
33 The Mall, Waterford
Town Bar & Grill, Dublin

• The Bridgestone 100 Best Restaurants in Ireland is arranged **ALPHABETICALLY, BY COUNTY** so it begins with County Cavan, which is followed by County Clare, and so on. Within the counties, the entries are once again listed alphabetically, so Good Things Café, in Durrus, West Cork, is followed by Les Gourmandises, in Cork city. Entries in Northern Ireland are itemised alphabetically, at the end of the book. All NI prices are quoted in sterling.

• The contents of the Bridgestone 100 Best Guides are exclusively the result of the authors' deliberations. All meals and accommodation were paid for and any offers of discounts or gifts were refused.

• Many of the places featured in this book are only open during the summer season, which means that they can be closed for any given length of time between October and March.

• **PRICES:** Dinner prices are calculated for an average three-course menu, without wine. Where the restaurant operates a set menu, that price is given.

• **LISTINGS:** In every entry in the book we try to list telephone number, (✆) fax, (🖷) and internet details (🖰). We also request details of disabled access(♿), the ability to cater for children, plus any other relevant details.

• **WEBSITES:** Where an entry has a website, we always print the address, as this is the place where you will find most up-to-date information concerning that listing. All the entries in all the Bridgestone Guides are linked then to www.bridgestoneguides.com, where you will find a food portal with all the best food addresses in Ireland.

• **BRIDGESTONE PLAQUES:** Look out for our Bridgestone Plaques, displayed by many of our listed establishments.

CONTENTS

INDEX

THE MacNEAN RESTAURANT

The Maguire family
Blacklion
County Cavan
℡ **071-985 3022**
🖷 **071-985 3404**
🖱 **www.macneanrestaurant.com**

Neven Maguire's red-hot MacNean Restaurant personifies all that is best about contemporary Irish cooking.

Neven Maguire and his crew are on a roll, right now, firing out irrepressibly delicious food for happy folk, and that is an important fact for the state of Irish cuisine, for a simple reason. Mr Maguire personifies the best aspects of Irish restaurant culture, in its modesty, its uniqueness, its generosity. He is not just cook, but also teacher, host, creator, ambassador and author. The many strands of the business are all brought together in his life and work, and the fact that he is so seamlessly and successfully assimilating all of those elements in such a positive way is pivotal to breeding a successful food culture.

Intellectual analysis aside, what Mr Maguire does is simply outstanding in terms of taste, appearance and originality: poached oyster with spinach and lemon foam; lamb in potato crust with braised lamb neck; john dory wrapped in courgette flower with wild asparagus; summer fruit trifle with raspberry ice cream; rhubarb mousse with balsamic ice cream. Tip-top cooking, and a red-hot address.

● **OPEN:** 6pm-9pm Wed-Sun; 1pm & 3.30pm Sun (closed Wed low season)
● **PRICE:** Sun Lunch €27, Dinner €55-€60
● **CREDIT CARDS:** Visa, Mastercard

● **NOTES:**
♿ access. Recommended for vegetarians, special menu.

● **DIRECTIONS:**
On the main street in Blacklion, in the centre of the village, which itself is just on the border with Northern Ireland.

THE BLACK OAK

Tom & Bernie Hamilton
Rineen
Miltown Malbay
County Clare
℡ **065-708 4403**
🖱 **www.blackoakclare.com**

Tom and Bernie Hamilton's Black Oak restaurant confidently delivers exactly what the menus promise. It's the people's choice, with ace value for money.

Eight years down the line, and Tom and Bernie Hamilton continue to do what they have always done: nice food, good value, good service, great views (so long as you book for the front room with the views over Liscannor Bay – this is important) and in a county where the gap between the promise of the menu and the reality of what ends up on the plate can be profound, we salute their modesty and commitment to consistency.

The cooking is modern and fun, with certain consistent signature dishes, such as the elaborate Black Oak salad or the speciality Seafood Pot, which mixes fresh fish and shellfish in a heady Spanish-accented brew – yes, that is saffron – served with sourdough bread. Fish is the star, but typically there are good vegetarian choices, and the broad span of the menu explains why the 'Oak is the locals' choice for many miles around. Cracking puddings are seriously rich and indulgent, the cherry on the cake of a professional operation that delivers what it promises.

● **OPEN:** 6pm-10pm, closed Sun-Mon.
Weekends only April & May, Oct-Dec.
Closed Jan-Mar.
● **PRICE:** Dinner €37
● **CREDIT CARDS:** Visa, Mastercard, Amex, Laser

● **NOTES:**
♿ access.

● **DIRECTIONS:**
5km south of Lahinch on the Miltown Malbay road, look for the sign on the left, going south.

CHERRY TREE RESTAURANT

Harry McKeogh
Lakeside, Ballina, Killaloe
County Clare
✆ **061-375688**
🖨 **071-375689**
🖱 **www.cherrytreerestaurant.ie**

Harry McKeogh and Mark
Anderson are poets of the
plate, crafting cultured dishes
with the skill of poets.

The Cherry Tree seems as well-established a fixture of
Irish gastronomy as many of the other entries in this
book that have been open for years, if not indeed
decades. So, it can come as a shock to realise that the CT
is only six years old, How to explain its sense of endur-
ing? Simply that this is a restaurant that practices first
principles: great sourcing of foods, great creative cooking,
sweet and lovely service. But Harry McKeogh and chef
Mark Anderson also have a romantic, indeed poetic con-
ception of their calling, they craft food like poets craft
lines: Bere Island scallops with Parmesan gnocchi, lemon
samphire and aged balsamic; halibut with a smoked haddock ballotine, pomme galette, pea purée and leek fon-
due; rhubarb and custard crème brulée scented with ginger with apple sorbet. This is crafted, stratified cooking,
the result of a patient method and of an artistic calling.
Right across the board, from first principles to final
executon, the CT is a benchmark modern Irish restaurant.

● **OPEN:** 6pm-10pm Tue-Sat , 12.30pm-3pm Sun
● **PRICE:** Dinner €39, (€70 gourmand - 10 courses),
Sun Lunch €24 two courses, €29 three courses.
● **CREDIT CARDS:** Visa, Mastercard, Amex, Laser

● **NOTES:**
♿ access. Recommended for vegetarians. Excellent children's menu (cooking with no bits, no skin & no bones)

● **DIRECTIONS:**
Drive through Ballina village, turn left towards the
bridge and right at Molly's pub, towards Lakeside Hotel.

BALLYMALOE HOUSE

The Allen family
Shanagarry, East Cork
✆ **021-465 2531**
🖷 **021-465 2021**
🖰 **www.ballymaloe.ie**

Ballymaloe House is riding
major kitchen changes with
confidence and ever-greater
success in this unique house.

Rory O'Connell has stepped back from the kitchen at
Ballymaloe House, and Jason Fahy's name now appears on
the menu as head chef. But, if you weren't given to study-
ing the fine print of the menu, you might not have guessed
that such a major change has taken place, for Mr Fahy is
continuing the Ballymaloe tradition of noble, simple cooking that uses the best local ingredients, served with
demure modesty. Dinner runs through five courses, from
celeriac and hazelnut soup, via a smashing dish of Tom's
glazed quail with sweet chilli peppers (well done, Tom,
excellent quail) to a winning main course of Gubbeen
ham with Chablis and cream with beetroot, then Irish
farmhouse cheeses and, finally, the splendid dessert trol-
ley with its timeless confections. Some might expect
more culinary histrionics, given the relatively high cost of
dinner. But that is not Mr Fahy's way, and it is not the
Ballymaloe way. Fashion isn't the issue here: goodness is
the issue, and graciousness is the issue, and both are well.

● **OPEN:** 7pm-9pm Mon-Sun 12.30pm-
1.30pm Sun
● **PRICE:** Lunch from €35, Dinner €62
● **CREDIT CARDS:** Visa, Mastercard, Amex

● **NOTES:**
♿ access. Early children's dinner.

● **DIRECTIONS:**
29km east of Cork city. Take the N25 to exit for
Whitegate R630, follow signs for R629 Cloyne. The
House is 3km beyond Cloyne, signposted.

10 RESTAURANTS
KIDS WILL LOVE

1

AROMA
DONEGAL, Co DONEGAL

2

CHERRY TREE RESTAURANT
KILLALOE, Co CLARE

3

THE DIM SUM RESTAURANT
BELFAST, Co ANTRIM

4

KINSALE GOURMET STORE
KINSALE, Co CORK

5

MACAU
BELFAST, Co ANTRIM

6

MACNEAN RESTAURANT
BLACKLION, Co CAVAN

7

THE MILL
DUNFANAGHY, Co DONEGAL

8

LA MARINE
ROSSLARE, Co WEXFORD

9

O'CONNELL'S
BALLSBRIDGE, Co DUBLIN

10

THE TANNERY
DUNGARVAN, Co WATERFORD

CAFÉ PARADISO

Denis Cotter & Bridget Healy
16 Lancaster Quay
Cork, County Cork
℗ **021-427 7939**
🖷 **021-427 4973**
🖰 **www.cafeparadiso.ie**

Denis Cotter cooks with
ingredients like an artist
using paint, turning abstrac-
tions into pure artworks.

Denis Cotter has simplified his lunch menus in Café
Paradiso during the past year, offering more small dishes
at lunchtime – risotto of roast parsnip and lemon with
parsley oil and Oisin cheese; red cabbage springroll with
green curry of cauliflower and tofu and lemongrass rice;
gratin of leeks and roasted roots with hazelnut and
Gabriel crust, sunchoke cream and braised fennel; dark
chocolate and pecan brownie with white chocolate ice
cream; sultana brioche bread & butter pudding with cinnamon custard and brandied orange marmalade syrup.
There is something interesting here amidst this delicious
roll-call of dishes: just look at the use of colour in this
food, look at how the use of ingredients can make these
dishes, which in culinary terms are completely abstract,
into vivid, colourful realities. That is one of the reasons
why Mr Cotter's cooking is unique: he sees the abstract
ingredients of food with a painter's eye, which explains
why he doesn't need to use meat. He is an artist.

- **OPEN:** 12pm-3pm, 6.30pm-10.30pm Tue-Sat
- **PRICE:** Lunch €23, Dinner €45
- **CREDIT CARDS:** Visa, Mastercard

- **NOTES:**
♿ access, but not to three rooms available for B&B.

- **DIRECTIONS:**
The Western Road leads away from Cork city centre to
the University area, and further west. Cafe Paradiso is
opposite the Lancaster Lodge, and is on your right as
you head away from the city.

CASINO HOUSE

Kerrin & Michael Relja
Coolmain Bay, Kilbrittain
West Cork
☎ **023-49944**
🖷 **021-49945**
✍ **chouse@eircom.net**

Strange ingredients are combined together in unusual ways in a manner that seems second nature to Michael Relja, of West Cork's Casino House.

"Cream of vegetable, pak choy and sesame oil soup".
Ah yes. That will be a starter dish by Michael Relja, from West Cork's Casino House, then.
That's what Mr Relja does that is so nice: he does what others don't do. Partly this is because he has such an impressive technique, so making mental leaps and unprecedented configurations with strange ingredients comes as second nature to him. He will put organic smoked salmon tartare into a tomato, something an Irish chef wouldn't dream of doing. He will add caraway seeds to a Burgundy sauce for fillet steak. He will confit a leg of rabbit then wrap it in prosciutto. Veal will have a sauce that has Dijon mustard – as expected – and a shot of maple syrup – as unexpected.
If it was simply done for the sake of it, it would be worthless. But the exposition of ingredients this cooking uncovers is great fun. The room is beautiful, and superbly managed by Kerrin Relja, and wines offer very good value.

● **OPEN:** 17 Mar-Dec, 7pm-9pm Mon-Sun, closed Wed; weekends only Nov-Dec; open Sun lunch.
● **PRICE:** Lunch €25, Dinner €40
● **CREDIT CARDS:** Visa, Mastercard, Amex

● **NOTES:**
♿ access. Gate Lodge cottage available to rent nightly/weekly €75 per night.

● **DIRECTIONS:**
On the R600 road between Timoleague & Kinsale. Casino House is signposted from Ballinspittle.

THE CRAWFORD GALLERY

Isaac Allen
Emmet Place
Cork
℡ **021-427 4415**
🖱 **www.ballymaloe.ie**

Isaac Allen has a pacific, harmonious style of cooking, which perfectly suits the calm of the Crawford Gallery, one of Cork city's finest dining rooms.

Isaac Allen has been a busy guy in recent times, choosing to open a pizza restaurant, Cibo, and The Bank, both close to his locus classicus, the Crawford Gallery. As the gallery is a daytime only restaurant, this has not created the tensions that might have happened to other chef-proprietors who try to take on the impossible feat of tri-location. So, for daytime, Mr Allen remains firmly in charge of The Crawford, one of the most beautiful and beloved places to eat in Cork city. Whilst he likes to add modern flourishes to his menus, for the most part they remain firmly embedded in the tradition and culture of great Cork cooking. Fish is fresh from Ballycotton, and is consistently a revelation, especially the fresh mackerel, and if Mr Allen has a signature it is with his consistent excellence with pies and braised dishes – he is a gentle, pacific cook, and thereby produces a style of food perfectly suited to this most genteel and timeless room in the Crawford. Great puds, and a great place for even the simplest bite.

● **OPEN:** 10am-4.30pm Mon-Fri; 9.30am-4pm Sat. Closed Sun
● **PRICE:** Lunch €24.50
● **CREDIT CARDS:** Visa, Mastercard, Amex, Diners

● **NOTES:**
♿ access.

● **DIRECTIONS:**
Around the corner from the Opera House, on a road that runs parallel to Patrick Street.

GOOD THINGS CAFÉ

Carmel Somers
Ahakista Road, Durrus
County Cork
℡ 027-61426
🖷 027-61426
🖰 www.thegoodthingscafe.com

The star of the county of West Cork, Carmel Somers' Good Things is the undisputed cream of the crop.

In just three short seasons, Carmel Somers has made Good Things Café the star of the County of West Cork. "From the outside, Good Things Café resembles nothing more grand than a village tearoom, enjoying quiet prospects of Dunmanus Bay, at what feels like the edge of the world – yet it is as if we are at the very centre of it", was how Howard Jacobson summarised his West Cork experience, and his words hint at why Ms Somers has made GTC such a success: she has made it the centre of the culinary culture of West Cork. The local foods are here – Gubbeen ham; Glenilen cream; Durrus cheese; Dunmanus Bay lobster; Bantry fresh fish; Murphy's ice cream; Schull vegetables – and in using these doorstep ingredients, Ms Somers has taken a food culture at the edge of Europe and turned it into the epicentre of contemporary Irish cooking. And, each year, the cooking has grown more confident, gaining poise, accuracy and deliciousness. Out of season, don't miss the cookery classes.

● **OPEN:** 10.30am-5pm, lunch served 12.30pm-4pm Wed-Mon; 7pm-8.30pm Fri-Mon; 7-days in August. Closed Jan-Mar. Weekends only off season.
● **PRICE:** Main Courses €11.50-€23.50
● **CREDIT CARDS:** Visa, Mastercard, Laser

● **NOTES:**
♿ access. Food to-go. Shop selling food, produce and cookery books. Cookery classes off season.

● **DIRECTIONS:**
On the Ahakista road just outside the village of Durrus.

LES GOURMANDISES

Patrick & Soizic Kiely
17 Cook Street
Cork
County Cork
✆ **021-425 1959**
⌂ **www.lesgourmandises.ie**

Patrick Kiely's cooking is like a chess game of flavours and textures, cerebral and intriguing. The made-over dining room is now very stylish.

They have remade the dining room in Les Gourmandises, and greatly improved it at that, so it's now a colourful, comfortable space. Pat Kiely's cooking, meanwhile, remains rock solid in technique and ambitious in intent. Here is a chef who lays out the entire palette of flavours and textures in every dish he sends out – an assiette of foie gras plays with every permutation of the liver; a tian of crab comes with a sauce gazpacho and a superb crab beignet, not to mention a ballotine of sole, offering contrasts on every front. John dory will have both wild mushrooms and asparagus, then a cep dressing and rich fondant potato. It's rich cooking – make sure you have a good appetite before dinner – but it's not showy or grandstanding. Instead, it's enthusiastic and generous cooking, and quite modest in its own way. Right to the end of dinner, when a Taste of Coffee brings you coffee parfait, chocolate and coffee pudding and gâteau opera, all of them flawlessly executed, Mr Kiely is over-delivering.

● **OPEN:** 6pm-10pm Tue-Sat
● **PRICE:** Dinner €39.50 for 3-course meal, served with glass of wine & coffee (served 6pm-10pm, Tue-Thu and 6pm-7pm, Fri). À la carte menu €39-€45.
● **CREDIT CARDS:** Visa, Mastercard, Laser

● **NOTES:**
♿ access, but not to toilets.

● **DIRECTIONS:**
Cook Street runs between Patrick Street and Oliver Plunkett Street, and the restaurant is half way down.

ISLAND COTTAGE

John Desmond & Ellmary Fenton
Heir Island, Skibbereen
West Cork
℡ **028-38102**
🖷 **021-38102**
🖱 **www.islandcottage.com**

Take the boat across to little Heir Island for one of Ireland's most unique, most memorable, food concepts.

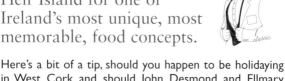

Here's a bit of a tip, should you happen to be holidaying in West Cork and should John Desmond and Ellmary Fenton's Island Cottage be one of your target destinations. The tip is this: get to the island early, by whatever means you can, and try to get in a spot of swimming and lazing on some of the fantastic beaches around the coast of Heir Island. White-sanded and deserted, they are a series of secret little coves that are a treat.

And now, invigorated by sea and sun, it is 8pm, and time for dinner, so stroll down to the Cottage, meet up with your friends, and prepare yourself for Mr Desmond's rigorous cooking and Ms Fenton's rigorous housekeeping. There is no choice on the menu, and it doesn't matter, for from chicken liver pâté on toast as you quaff your drinks through to glorious fish cookery, local duck cooked as well as any Frenchman could manage, and heavenly, light puddings, the food will be captured in your memory as part of one of Ireland's most unique food experiences.

● **OPEN:** 8pm-midnight, 15 June-15 Sept, Wed-Sat
● **PRICE:** Dinner €40
● **CREDIT CARDS:** No credit cards

● **NOTES:**
Booking absolutely essential. Not suitable for children.
No vegetarians or special diets catered for. No deviation from set menu. Cookery courses off season.

● **DIRECTIONS:**
The shortest ferry trip is from Cunnamore pier, which is signposted to Hare Island off the N71.

IVORY TOWER

Seamus O'Connell
The Exchange Buildings
Princes Street
Cork, County Cork
© **021-427 4665**
🖰 **www.seamusoconnell.com**

Seamus O'Connell works endless themes and variations on his favourite ingredients and dishes, always improvising wildly with new hot new ideas.

Here is what we would like to do with Seamus O'Connell. Take a radio programme, à la Anthony Clare's In The Psychiatrist's Chair, and let Mr O'Connell lie down, and then analyse a menu, with the man answering how he dreamed up his dishes.

Okay, Seamus: guinea and popcorn broth with Asian greens, how did that come about? Bouillabaisse of gurnard: why? back in 1996 you served mallard with sherry and a white peach demijus, but nowadays the mallard come with vanilla, sherry and jalapenos, how did that shift occur, and why? Why the saffron in the crème brûlée?

The answers would reveal a culinary mind that is polyglot but which is in no way promiscuous. Many of Mr O'Connell's dishes have been served for ten or more years, but the point about the Ivory Tower is that the dishes are always shifting, changing, assimilating new themes and obsessions. That is why, for some, it is the most exciting food you can eat. Others just don't get it.

● **OPEN:** 6.30pm-midnight Wed-Sat., from 11.30am Mon-Sat.
● **PRICE:** Dinner €60-€75, Lunch mains €10-€15
● **CREDIT CARDS:** Visa, Mastercard, Amex

● **NOTES:**
Private dining room. Japanese menu every Tuesday. Cookery demos Wed-Thur.

● **DIRECTIONS:**
Up the stairs, on the corner of Princes Street and Oliver Plunkett Street.

JACOB'S ON THE MALL

Tom & Kate McCarthy
30a South Mall,
Cork, County Cork
☎ **021-425 1530**
🖷 **021-425 1531**
🖱 **www.jacobsonthemall.com**

From dry martinis to baked Alaska, Mercy Fenton and her sharp crew deliver the full experience in Jacob's.

The secret of Jacob's is to start right at the beginning: order a gin martini, for they know how to make a truly dry, arresting cocktail in here. Now, take it from there: lamb patties with hot and sour salad to start shows how this kitchen can take the simplest of ideas and make them seem as profound as poetry. Then, chicken with colcannon and spinach shows how Mercy Fenton and her crew do the very best Irish comfort food you can get, using superb ingredients and, again, making something seem seem profound, thanks to understanding how every element of the dish contributes to its overall success. Rhubarb food in tuile with ginger ice cream is a little game with expected ideas and textures, and is just as successful as everything else: the fried polenta with tomato pesto, purple-sprouting broccoli and oven-dried tomatoes, the charred salmon with short-grain rice in coconut milk, the fun baked Alaska. Life is simply too short to take Jacob's on the Mall at anything other than the full A-Z

● **OPEN:** 12.30pm-2.30pm, 6.30pm-10pm Mon-Sat. Closed Sun
● **PRICE:** Lunch €32.50, Dinner €45
● **CREDIT CARDS:** Visa, Mastercard, Amex, Diners

● **NOTES:**
♿ access.

● **DIRECTIONS:**
A south city centre restaurant, at the Grand Parade end of South Mall. The restaurant is next to the bank and just behind the main post office. Discreetly signposted.

JACQUES

**Jacqueline Barry &
Eithne Barry**
Phoenix Street, Cork, County Cork
℮ **021-427 7387**
🖷 **021-427 0634**
🖰 **www.jacquesrestaurant.ie**

Jacq and Eithne Barry have run a hip restaurant for 26 years, all the while staying hip to the trip themselves, and serving great contemporary cooking.

Why and how has Jacq and Eithne Barry's restaurant survived and thrived for 26 years? Simple: because people love it. Everyone has restaurants they use, and restaurants they like. But then there is a small group or class of restaurant that people love, that they take to their heart, that feeds more than their body, in some strange way. Jacques is one of those restaurants. In fact, it is one of those restaurants that it is great fun to introduce newcomers to, and to see their reaction to the room, the service, the style. Quickly, you find that they have been back on their own, maybe to have just some duck livers on polenta and chicken satay with pilaff rice from the early bird menu, or perhaps a quick lunch of crispy duck and watercress salad and then crab and lemon cannelloni. And, suddenly, they are telling you just what an excellent wine list Jacques has (quite right) and how they always start with a glass of manzanilla and how their fave pudding is now the lime and coconut parfait.. Another fan.

● **OPEN:** noon-3pm Mon-Fri; 6pm-10pm Mon-Sat; 5pm-9pm Sun
● **PRICE:** Lunch from €15.90, Dinner €45
● **CREDIT CARDS:** Visa, Mastercard, Amex

● **NOTES:**
Early Bird dinner, 2-course, 6pm-7pm Mon-Sat, €19.90. Outside catering for small or large parties available. See website for more details.

● **DIRECTIONS:**
Just behind the main post office in the centre of the city.

10 RESTAURANTS
FOR GREAT ROMANCE

1
CHAPTER ONE
DUBLIN, Co DUBLIN

2
COAST
TRAMORE, Co WATERFORD

3
GOOD THINGS CAFÉ
DURRUS, Co CORK

4
JAMES STREET SOUTH
BELFAST, Co ANTRIM

5
LONGUEVILLE HOUSE
MALLOW, Co CORK

6
MOSSIE'S
ADRIGOLE, Co CORK

7
RATHMULLAN HOUSE
RATHMULLAN, Co DONEGAL

8
TODDIE'S
KINSALE, Co CORK

9
TOWN BAR & GRILL
DUBLIN, Co DUBLIN

10
SHU
BELFAST, Co ANTRIM

KINSALE GOURMET STORE

Martin & Marie Shanahan
The Guardwell
Kinsale
West Cork
✆ **021-477 4453**

Kinsale's unique fish restaurant charms and delights everyone, from critics to chefs to hungry punters.

"The whole Fishy Fishy experience, over which owner Martin Shanahan presides like a shop foreman, with a pencil behind his ear, is permeated with the down-to-earth energy of the town: open kitchen, bare tables, people coming in to gossip and a counter selling fresh fish to take out... how Fishy Fishy manages to feel so local without being in the least parochial is its secret."

The writer and novelist Howard Jacobson, who wrote the above in New York's *Food & Wine* magazine, speculated that Mr Shanahan's secret was several years cooking in San Francisco: "The chowder has more coriander in it than you would expect on this side of the world... the john dory hints of somewhere more exotic than the Atlantic, its tangy fresh-tomato sauce tasting of the Mediterranean". That is a super analysis of Mr Shanahan's style: he has fused influences and experiences and seamlessly re-presented them as his signature. And with a new Fishy Fishy planned for 2006, down near Acton's, it's all go.

● **OPEN:** noon-4pm (shop open 9am-5.30pm)
● **PRICE:** Lunch €25-€29
● **CREDIT CARDS:** No credit cards accepted

● **NOTES:**
♿ access, but not to toilets.

● **DIRECTIONS:**
Take the airport road out of Cork, follow signs for Kinsale. The restaurant is next to St Multose church, in the section of Kinsale known as the Guardwell, just at the north end of the town.

LONGUEVILLE HOUSE

The O'Callaghan family
The President's Restaurant
Mallow, North Cork
📞 **022-47156**
🖨 **022-47459**
🖱 **www.longuevillehouse.ie**

Since his first appearance in the Bridgestones, William O'Callaghan's culinary journey has never ceased.

Most chefs hit a creative peak at an early point in their career and then, from that point on, they coast. Their food stays much the same, but it rarely keeps moving forward, the experimentation tends to flatten.

William O'Callaghan is one of those rare cooks who bucks that trend. He appeared in the first Bridgestone Irish Food Guide back in 1991, but what has characterised his work ever since is the simple fact that he has never stood still. Every season, every year, brings new inventions, new creations, new ways of working with and thinking about food. In 1992 Longueville lamb was baked in a potato crust and served with its juices; today, Longueville lamb is served as a mosaic, with a gâteau of aubergine and tomato and a rosemary sauce; Blackwater salmon is today served as a carpaccio with sorrel pesto, back then it was served en papillote with garden vegetables. Best of all, you can taste and enjoy this singular cook's culinary journey in every single thing he cooks.

- **OPEN:** 6.30pm-8.30pm Mon-Sun
- **PRICE:** Dinner €55-€75
- **CREDIT CARDS:** All major cards accepted

- **NOTES:**
Limited ♿ access.
Recommended for vegetarians.

- **DIRECTIONS:**
5km from Mallow in direction of Killarney. Pass racecourse on left, and shortly after you will see sign for Longueville House.

MOSSIE'S

David & Lorna Ramshaw
Trafrask, Adrigole, Beara
West Cork
℡ **027-60606**
🖱 **www.mossiesrestaurant.com**

David and Lorna Ramshaw
are the latest mavericks to
open a stylish restaurant on
the distant Beara peninsula.

Mossie's is the latest maverick West Cork arrival to showcase the talents and aesthetic of a talented couple. A delightful restaurant with rooms in the pretty Ulusker House, a few miles just north-west of Adrigole on the Beara Peninsula, it has the triple-stimulant of charming, subtle rooms, a stylish and popular restaurant, and a smashing garden surrounded by mature trees.

The cooking is not the cutting edge variety of other West Cork addresses such as Good Things or the much-missed Customs House, but Lorna Renshaw and her team assemble a careful, composed and colourful style of domestic cooking that suits the space – and its punters – perfectly: crab and smoked salmon salad; tomato and basil soup; monkfish wrapped in Parma ham with lemon and rosemary; grilled lemon sole with asparagus and shrimp; a plosive, colourful summer pudding. Value is very keen, and at the weekends the room is alight with energy and style and the buzz of a local audience. A great new arrival.

● **OPEN:** noon-3.30pm Lunch, 3.30pm-6pm Tea, 7pm-9.30pm Dinner. Closed Mon & Tues during low season.
● **PRICE:** Dinner €34, Lunch in the garden €12, Sunday lunch €20
● **CREDIT CARDS:** Visa, Mastercard, Laser

● **NOTES:**
♿ access. Rates available for dinner, B&B & Sun lunch.

● **DIRECTIONS:**
12 minutes from Glengarrif. Follow the Castletownbere road, and look for signs just before Adrigole.

O'CALLAGHAN-WALSHE

Sean Kearney
The Square, Rosscarbery
West Cork
✆ **023-48125**
🖷 **021-48125**
🖱 **funfish@indigo.ie**

Fresh, wild fish from
Atlantic waters cooked and
served with sympathy and
skill is the O'C-W formula.

In the modern restaurant world, great restaurants no
longer give the public what the public wants.

Instead, they do something much more radical, and sensi-
ble. They give the public what they can do best.

Look at how this works in O'Callaghan-Walshe, a restaurant that sounds like a firm of solicitors and that looks
like a pub with an interior that looks like a stage set. And
here, Martina O'Donovan produces some of the best fish
cookery you can eat, sourced from the Atlantic by local
boats: fresh prawns with garlic and lemon; fishcakes with
chermoula; big prawn scampi; wild Kerry sea bass with
peperonata; Rosscarbery lobster grilled; brill with shellfish sauce. Ms O'Donovan's fish cookery is then served
with witty insouciance by the quietly humorous Sean
Kearney. True, there is a fillet steak, and a duck confit
spring roll but otherwise it is wild fish, cooked with wild
skill and served with wild wit. That's what they do, they do
it brilliantly, and that's why O'C-W is so radical.

● **OPEN:** 6.30pm-9.30pm Tue-Sun. Weekends only Oct-
May
● **PRICE:** Dinner €45
● **CREDIT CARDS:** Visa, Mastercard, Laser

● **NOTES:**
♿ access, but not to toilets. Reservations recommended.
Chefs would prefer if vegetarians prebooked.

● **DIRECTIONS:**
On the main square in Rosscarbery. In the centre of
Rosscarbery. Turn off at the Celtic Ross hotel.

OTTO'S CREATIVE CATERING

Hilda & Otto Kunze
Dunworley, Butlerstown
Bandon
West Cork
✆ **023-40461**
🖰 **www.ottoscreativecatering.com**

Otto's Creative Catering is
a place in which you can
understand the timeless
nature of great cooking.

"Otto Kunze is dedicated to finding and using the best
ingredients possible, and in his hands they are crafted into
the finest recipes one could imagine".
We wrote that way, way back, in our first book, in 1989.
Times have changed. Ireland has changed. West Cork,
even West Cork, has changed.
But Otto Kunze has not changed.
OCC offers the best ingredients you can eat, transformed
into the finest dishes you can eat. It offers these local
foods, from wild herbs, leaves and garden vegetables to
fish and local meats, in a bespoke environment where Mr
Kunze takes the art of cooking and eating into a different
world, a place where the goodness of the food achieves
holistic transcendence. No other cooking tastes like this,
no other cooking has a philosophy as deeply rooted as
this. And that is because Otto and Hilda Kunze have never
changed. They do what they do, they work the way they
work, because they believe in what they do. Timeless.

● **OPEN:** 7pm-9.30pm Wed-Sat & Sun lunch, 1.30pm
● **PRICE:** Lunch €35, Dinner €50
● **CREDIT CARDS:** Visa, Mastercard, Laser, Maestro

● **NOTES:**
Reservations only. You can bring your own wine if you
wish. Accommodation €60 per person sharing. ♿ access
to dining room.

● **DIRECTIONS:**
From Bandon go to Timoleague, follow signs to
Barryroe until you come across signs to Dunworley.

TODDIE'S
@ THE KINSALE BREWERY

Pearse & Mary O'Sullivan
The Glen, Kinsale,
West Cork
✆ **021-477 7769**
🖥 **www.toddieskinsale.com**

Pearse and Mary O'Sullivan's Toddie's is now smack bang in the centre of Kinsale, and smack bang at the centre of modern, creative Irish cookery.

Toddie's has moved – down into the heart of Kinsale – and already Pearse and Mary O'Sullivan are the talk of the town, with Mrs O'Sullivan magisterially in charge of the fine space that used to be the Kinsale Brewing Company, whilst Mr O'Sullivan is happily showing everyone just what a red-hot culinary talent he is.

That talent was always evident, but the move into a funkier, more modern room – which has a peachy verandah for days when the sun shines – has led to new energy and pizazz. Crab cake with guacamole and Asian pesto; hake with fennel purée, chilli, lime and coriander buttered clams; ravioli of lobster and saffron with cherry tomato butter; lemon and lime tart; chocolate and orange crème brûlée. Lunch has a punky wholemeal pizza with Ardsallagh cheese and artichoke hearts, and a bumper seafood platter. This is the food locals and visitors to Kinsale have wanted to eat for a long time, and a new star has arrived: this is Mr O'Sullivan's time, so don't miss it.

● **OPEN:** 6.30pm-10.30pm Tue-Sun, Mon-Sun high season, closed Mon low season. Closed Jan.
● **PRICE:** Dinner €45
● **CREDIT CARDS:** Visa, Mastercard, Amex

● **NOTES:**
♿ access.

● **DIRECTIONS:**
From the centre of Kinsale, looking up towards the White House restaurant, turn right. Toddie's is two doors along, upstairs, through the brewery gates.

AROMA

Tom Dooley & Arturo de Alba
Donegal Craft Village
Donegal
County Donegal
℡ 074-972 3222

The most perfect dish we ate in 2005? White wine risotto with asparagus, cooked in the tiny Aroma.

Aroma is tiny, and modestly describes itself as a "Coffee Shop & Mini Bakery". Do not be deceived. Tom and Arturo knock out food for the gods in this minuscule space, continuing the tradition of other great small places to eat in Ireland – Grangecon, Fishy Fishy, Good Things, to name but three other don't miss wee addresses.

Small it may be, but the focus is pin-point sharp. That dish of risotto with fresh asparagus and white wine and Parmesan, for example, was delivered better than any other dish we enjoyed in 2005, and 2005 was a bumper year. Everything about the dish was faultless, so fine you could have believed that a team of six had laboured over it. But, it only needed Arturo de Alba to make it perfectly. The rest of his cooking is similarly focused: tomato, pear and ginger soup (wild!); chicken, mushroom and garlic casserole; prawn and avocado salad. The lovely daytime eating is congratulated by Tom Dooley's expert sweet cakes and breads, and the staff are spot on. A (little) star.

- **OPEN:** 9.30am-5.30pm Tue-Sat (7 days in season)
- **PRICE:** Lunch €16.50
- **CREDIT CARDS:** No credit cards accepted.

- **NOTES:**
  ♿ access.

- **DIRECTIONS:**
Take the old road directly into Donegal town, avoiding the new bypass. The Craft Village is a collection of single storey craft workshops south of the town and clearly signposted, 2km or so outside the town.

THE MILL RESTAURANT

Derek & Susan Alcorn
Figart, Dunfanaghy
North Donegal
✆ **074-913 6985**
🖷 **074-913 6985**
🖰 **www.themillrestaurant.com**

Rip Off Ireland? No one
seems to have told The
Mill that they shouldn't be
offering unbeatable value.

In a piece of journalism written for *The Irish Independent*
in mid-2005 we tried to point out a simple truism about
modern Irish restaurants: where you find the best food is
also usually where you will find the best value.

And who was our champion example of this truth? The
Mill, that's who. Derek and Susan Alcorn offer outstanding value for money for outstanding cooking and service.
Best of all, the value also extends to their superb rooms,
so don't be discouraged by the trip all the way up north
to distant Dunfanaghy.

What you will discover there is one of the sharpest,
sweetest Irish restaurants, and great, inspired cooking –
Doe Castle mussels with garlic and cream; a subtle wild
mushroom and rosemary soup; fillet of beef with pearl
barley risotto and rösti potatoes; strawberry and white
chocolate parfait with summer berries. Derek Alcorn's
style is subtle yet pronounced, very focused on getting
the best flavours every time. Fantastic food, amazing value.

- **OPEN:** 7pm-9pm Tue-Sun
- **PRICE:** Dinner €38
- **CREDIT CARDS:** Visa, Mastercard, Amex

- **NOTES:**
♿ access. Recommended for children, excellent menu.

- **DIRECTIONS:**
Dunfanaghy is at the very tip of the country, coming up
to Horn Head. From L'kenny, take N56 through
Dunfanaghy. The Mill is situated 1km past the village on
right-hand side, beside New Lake.

RATHMULLAN HOUSE

The Wheeler family
Lough Swilly, Rathmullan,
County Donegal
✆ **074-9158188**
🖷 **074-9158200**
🖱 **www.rathmullanhouse.com**

Local foods are used with stunning effect by Peter Cheesman in Rathmullan's dynamic, creative kitchen.

For very many happy folk, Rathmullan is the personification of a family-run, private, quiet, country house hotel. It's location is jaw-droppingly fine, the staff are superb, the comfort is understated, and the Wheeler family oversee it with genial grace and patient assurance. It's not cheap, but nor is it exorbitantly expensive. It's a treat.

But there is more than that to Rathmullan. It's not a smart but shaggy pile. This house is focused: they are members of Slow Food, their food is sourced locally and the cooking from Peter Cheesman, in particular, shows the mettle of this handsome house. This is a chef whose signature crab dish is an amazing confection of five separate ways to prepare crab, and it is genuinely unmissable. But then everything coming out of this kitchen, from lamb shank and beetroot terrine or a soup or Orla potatoes and thyme with foie gras, through to slow-braised shoulder of lamb of Mossbrook Farm cured belly and loin of pork, is gorgeous to look at, and even better to eat. A hot spot.

● **OPEN:** 7.30pm-8.45pm, (till 9pm Fri-Sat) Mon-Sun (mid-week and weekends only off season)
● **PRICE:** Dinner €50
● **CREDIT CARDS:** All major credit cards accepted.

● **NOTES:**
♿ access. Children especially welcome.

● **DIRECTIONS:**
From Rathmullan, go left at Mace store, follow the road past the Catholic Church, then past big black gates. Rathmullan House is at the end of this avenue.

AQUA RESTAURANT

Richard Clery & Charlie Smith
1 West Pier
Howth, County Dublin
℡ **01-832 0690**
🖷 **01-832 0687**
🖱 **www.aqua.ie**

Is Howth all set to be the next Shrewsbury Road for property fixated Dubliners? Well, if viewing properties, make sure your trip takes in Aqua.

With a Sunday farmers' market, the new Skye bar, a clutch of new shops and a near-completed harbour development about to get up-and-running, Howth seems to be taking its place amongst the groovy and happenings zones of Dublin. The good news for those who may be tempted to the northside bourgeois haven is that Aqua is, and has been, as steady-as-she-goes a restaurant as there has been in Dublin over the last several years.

They don't get a great deal of attention, but they do things nicely, producing modern food which is light and pleasing in a good room with professional service and great views out over the wee bay. Start with a solid-sender such as the calamari with spicy tomato sauce and roasted garlic, move on to some smoked chicken linguini with wild mushrooms, finish with a classic sticky toffee pudding with a glass of Banyuls, and all of a sudden you might find yourself dreamily and happily contemplating a pricey waterfront property in hip, happening Howth.

- **OPEN:** 1pm-3pm, 5.30pm-midnight, Mon-Sat; 12.30pm-4pm, 6pm-9.30pm Sun & Bank hols
- **PRICE:** Lunch €29.95, Dinner €40-€50
- **CREDIT CARDS:** Visa, Mastercard, Amex

- **NOTES:**
Bank holidays, open 6pm-9.30pm. Early Bird 5.30pm-7pm Tue-Fri, 5.30pm-6.30pm Sat €29.95

- **DIRECTIONS:**
On the west pier in Howth, from the DART station, turn left and follow to the end of the pier (5mins' walk).

BANG CAFÉ

Chris & Simon Stokes
11 Merrion Row
Dublin 2
℡ **01-676 0898**
🖷 **01-676 0899**
🖰 **www.bangrestaurant.com**

Chef Lorcan Gribbin and owners the Stokes brothers have kept the solid, reliable, and enjoyable formula of Bang Café right on the money.

It is a sign of his maturity and his confidence in his craft that Lorcan Gribbin, a chef with a masterly technique, never, ever cooks food that shows off, that grandstands the sort of fancy stuff he is actually capable of cooking. The result is that Bang is rock-sold and reliable, the kind of sure-bet restaurant every city needs in spades.

Bang reminds us of Rowley Leigh's Kensington Place, albeit on a much smaller scale, but what we mean is that the focus is on the food and the customer's satisfaction, the result of a team working confidently within their ability, but never allowing themselves to coast or take it easy. Some folk don't get Bang, because they focus on the socialite behaviour of the Stokes brothers, who own the place. Well, let them miss out, whilst you enjoy double-rib lamb chops with garlic confit, or scallops with mousseline potatoes and pancetta, or monkfish with butternut squash risotto, or a fine bitter and sweet Seville orange meringue pie. Lovely, grown-up, sophisticated cooking.

● **OPEN:** 12.30pm-3pm Mon-Sat; 6pm-10.30pm Mon-Wed; 6pm-11pm Thu-Sat. Closed Sun
● **PRICE:** Lunch €30, Dinner €45
● **CREDIT CARDS:** Visa, Mastercard, Amex

● **NOTES:**
No ♿ access.

● **DIRECTIONS:**
The restaurant is just beyond St Stephen's Green, beside the Bank of Ireland cash machine, where the road narrows.

CAVISTON'S

Peter Caviston
59 Glasthule Road, Sandycove
Dun Laoghaire, County Dublin
℡ 01-280 9245
🖷 01-284 4054
🖱 www.cavistons.com

Ask your Dublin friends which restaurant is their favourite place to have lunch. Caviston's, we'll bet.

Take a straw poll of your Dublin friends and acquaintances, asking them about their favourite places to eat lunch, and we will bet you a euro to a cent that Caviston's of Glasthule will emerge, very quickly, as the favourite destination of the metropolitan food lovers. Everyone loves it, and it is easy to see why.

The food, the service, the value, the clamorous ambience, the gentility and the urgency are all here in perfect balance; the working of the room as finely balanced as their superb fish and shellfish cookery. They haven't changed a thing since they opened – they just cook the freshest fish and shellfish, and they do it for three frantically busy lunch sittings a day, and no one minds the tight time frame in which you have to eat lunch, for everyone is too happy, too distracted with the delight of being in Caviston's. It is a great idea and a great concept but, even better, it is a great reality. That's why the metropolitan food lovers will travel, anytime, anytime, any excuse, to Glasthule.

● **OPEN:** three lunch sittings per day: noon, 1.30pm, 3pm Tue-Fri; noon, 1.45pm, 3.15pm Sat
● **PRICE:** Lunch €40
● **CREDIT CARDS:** All major cards accepted

● **NOTES:**
Reservations essential.

● **DIRECTIONS:**
Sandycove is a village south of the city centre and Caviston's is in the centre of the village, beside Caviston's Deli.

CHAPTER ONE

Ross Lewis & Martin Corbett
18-19 Parnell Square,
Dublin 1
℅ **01-873 2266**
🖷 **01-873 2330**
🖱 **www.chapteronerestaurant.com**

The best of restaurants, the
most modest of restaurants,
Chapter One is one of the
glories of Dublin dining.

Great metropolitan restaurants are usually reckoned to
be all about swagger, power and panache. It seems, however, that no one has told the Chapter One team that
they are supposed to be brash and boisterous.

These guys are so modest, so professional, so unassum-
ing, that you might find it hard to believe that they are
powering one of the busiest, most successful, most
dynamic and best-loved restaurants in the entire country,
or that they effortlessly combine a magnificent cocktail of
the best cooking and the best service. They just get on
with it, taking stellar standards for granted.

With Garret Byrne operating alongside Ross Lewis in the
kitchen, the food in Chapter One is spellbinding, from the
rustic, mellow lamb hot pot of loin and slow-cooked
shoulder with white beans to the fine purity of monkfish
with pea purée, sauté girolles and truffle foam. They may
not be brash at C1, but their confidence is wondrous to
behold, and the energy of the room is just mesmerising.

● **OPEN:** 12.30pm-2.30pm Tue-Fri; 6pm-11pm Tue-Sat;
6pm-10.30pm Tue-Sat
● **PRICE:** Dinner €52.50
● **CREDIT CARDS:** All major cards accepted

● **NOTES:**
Limited ♿ access - basement restaurant.
Pre-theatre, 6pm-7pm, €32 + 10% service (starter, main
course, then come back for dessert).

● **DIRECTIONS:**
In the basement of the Dublin Writers' Museum.

CHINA HOUSE

Gerry or Pearl (manager & supervisor)
180 Parnell Street
Dublin 1
☏ **01-873 3870**

Now housed in glamorous
new premises on Parnell
Street, China House offers
the most echt ethnic eating.

The big news from the heart of ethnic Dublin (Moore
Street) is that the China House has moved to a salubri-
ous (relatively speaking) two-storey premises on Parnell
Street. The new premises has two floors with about seven
tables on each level, the menu has lengthened, so off you
go: prawn crackers, steamed meat buns, Chinese chive
dumplings, folded crispy pancakes with pork and chives
and scallion pancake, and that's just for starters.

For mains, order the whole steamed fish with ginger and
scallions, and maybe stir-fried pork with dried mushrooms, peppers and onions in a savoury sweet and sour
style sauce which has a lovely lightness of touch, or check
out the sauté guts with tripe, pigs ears with scallions or
jellyfish skin with mature vinegar. Ace ethnic cooking.

Clientele are mostly Chinese, service is a little erratic but
very charming and do try to find a spot upstairs if you can
as the strip lighting downstairs is a little harsh. Rip off
Ireland? No-one told them in The China House.

- **OPEN:** 11am-12am Mon-Sun
- **PRICE:** Dinner €20
- **CREDIT CARDS:** No credit cards.

- **NOTES:**
Limited ♿ access - but would be happy to help.
Take-away service available.

- **DIRECTIONS:**
Parnell Street is at the northern end of O'Connell
Street and is home to many ethnic shops and restau-
rants. China House is at number 180.

DUNNE & CRESCENZI

Stefano Crescenzi & Eileen Dunne
16 South Frederick Street
Dublin 2
℃ **01-677 3815**
🖰 **www.dunneandcrescenzi.com**

With the brand new Nonna Valentina in Portobello, the D&C empire has gone into overdrive, producing mighty Italian food all over the city of Dublin.

Dunne & Crescenzi is only one element of Eileen Dunne and Stefano Crescenzi's pioneering Dublin food empire, which includes the three D&C's along with Bar Italia, La Corte, and the brand new Nonna Valentina, in Dublin's Portobello, where Stefano Crescenzi gets a chance to indulge his expertise and passion for traditional Italian cooking. To be honest, you can choose any of their addresses, and what you will get is happy food, simple food, and food served with grace and humour. Dunne & Crescenzi are fast becoming the Italian Avoca, and that is the highest compliment we can pay them. That means their restaurants are creative, direct and unpretentious, the food is properly understood, and careful attention is paid to every detail, whether you are having a plate of antipasti, a pasta dish in Sth Frederick Street at 10pm at night, or some tortino di patate in Portobello. We remember the little shop in Sutton where it began and where we first wrote about D&C. Acorns to mighty oaks.

● **OPEN:** 9am-11pm Mon-Sat, noon-7pm Sun
● **PRICE:** Meals from €10
● **CREDIT CARDS:** All major cards accepted

● **NOTES:**
Reservations only taken for parties of six or more (in which case minimum order €25 per person applies)

● **DIRECTIONS:**
South Frederick Street runs off Nassau Street in Dublin city centre, round the corner from Trinity College.

10 RESTAURANTS
TO BE SEEN IN

1

THE BALLYMORE INN
BALLYMORE EUSTACE, Co KILDARE

2

EDEN
DUBLIN, Co DUBLIN

3

FRANK'S BAR & RESTAURANT
DUBLIN, Co DUBLIN

4

GOOD THINGS CAFÉ
DURRUS, CO CORK

5

MACAU
BELFAST, Co ANTRIM

6

MACKEREL
DUBLIN, Co DUBLIN

7

MINT
DUBLIN, Co DUBLIN

8

RATHMULLAN HOUSE
RATHMULLAN, Co DONEGAL

9

33 THE MALL
WATERFORD, Co WATERFORD

10

TOWN BAR & GRILL
DUBLIN, Co DUBLIN

L'ECRIVAIN

Derry & Sallyanne Clarke
109 Lower Baggot Street
Dublin 2
℅ **01-661 1919**
🖷 **01-661 0617**
🖰 **www.lecrivain.com**

Derry and Sallyanne Clarke's L'Ecrivain restaurant defines contemporary Dublin dining right now.

How did Derry and Sallyanne Clarke do it? How did they go from being professional chefs and restaurateurs, to being first among equals? How did they manage to raise their game into another league? And how, having done that, have they managed to maintain their status as Dublin's outstanding restaurant, where L'Ecrivain defines the experience of contemporary eating in Dublin city.
We confess; we don't know. But we suspect two things are most important. One, Mr Clarke loves food. He is by nature an epicurean, and all the pleasure he finds in food is bundled up in his cooking. Secondly, he is such a genial chap that we reckon he doesn't get 110% from his staff; he gets 210%. And that is why L'Ecrivain is such a power-house experience, a world-class restaurant that would fit comfortably into any capital city anywhere in the world. Yes, it's very expensive to eat here now, but it's worth it, because the entire experience is so memorable, so glamorous, so stylish. The Clarkes are, simply, the guv'nors.

● **OPEN:** 12.30pm-2pm Mon-Fri; 7pm-11pm Mon-Sat
● **PRICE:** Lunch €35-€45, Dinner from €70
● **CREDIT CARDS:** Visa, Amex, Mastercard, Laser

● **NOTES:**
♿ access. on ground floor. Service charge on food only (10%)

● **DIRECTIONS:**
L'Ecrivain is located through a small archway, just beside Lad Lane, and across the road from the Bank of Ireland headquarters on Baggot Street.

EDEN

Jay Bourke & Eoin Foyle
Meeting House Square
Temple Bar, Dublin 2
℡ **01-670 5372**
🖷 **01-670 3330**
🖱 **www.edenrestaurant.ie**

Eden has rediscovered the
path to its holy grail, and
re-emerged as a smart
Dublin dining choice.

Eden's career trajectory has beeen the quintessentially
metropolitan journey. It opened with a bang, and pro-
ceeded to be the hippest hotspot in what was then the
radical and emerging Temple Bar project. As Temple Bar
settled down – or waned down, depending on your point
of view – Eden lost its groove and its focus, and service,
in particular, failed to deliver the potential of the room
and the location and the food.

But now, Eden is back where it belongs: a restaurant of
choice that figures amongst the smart choices in Dublin
for entertaining, and for having a good experience.
Michael Durkan's cooking capitalises on tasty modern
dishes – Eden smokies, carpaccio of beef with rocket,
lemon oil and Parmesan; beef and Guinness stew; fennel
risotto; duck confit with spiced plums; a fine chocolate
soufflé – and everything in the funky room has found its
measure and its focus. They have refound the will to do
well what they do well, and it makes for a happy room.

- **OPEN:** 12.30pm-3pm Mon-Fri; noon-3pm Sat & Sun;
6pm-10.30pm Mon-Sun
- **PRICE:** Lunch €19.50-€23, Dinner from €70
- **CREDIT CARDS:** Visa, Amex, Mastercard, Laser

- **NOTES:**
♿ access on ground floor. Special Dietary requirements
catered for with advance notice.

- **DIRECTIONS:**
Meeting House Square is between Eustace Street and
Dame Street in the heart of Temple Bar.

ELY

Erik Robson & Michelle Moyles
22 Ely Place
Dublin 2
℡ **01-676 8986**
🖷 **01-661 7288**
🖰 **www.elywinebar.ie**

Erik Robson & Michelle Moyles' Ely
is one of the key addresses in Dublin
city, with the best wine list, fine
organic food, and a great service crew.

"What we are doing here is really quite simple: giving our
customers a comfortable and relaxed environment in
which to enjoy drinking great wines and eating good honest food with the minimum of fuss and pretension... Our
ethos is to make sure that everything we do, we do well."
That's the problem with Erik and Michelle of Ely; they can
define and describe their modus operandi better than any
critic. They make the critics redundant.

Even better, they not only define their m.o.: they execute
it with the same intellectual and professional precision
that is apparent in their mission statement. Food, wines
and service are delivered by a crack team who relish their
work, creating what is simply one of the most atmospheric and enjoyable rooms in which to relax in the city.
At Bridgestone central we have a mantra that the truffled
lobster is no better than the ham sandwich made with
TLC, and Ely veritably defines that approach. ELY means
TLC, and so every little thing they do is magic.

● **OPEN:** noon-4pm Mon-Fri; 6pm-10pm Mon-Wed;
6pm-11pm Thur-Fri; 1pm-11pm Sat. Closed Sun.
● **PRICE:** Lunch €22, Dinner €35
● **CREDIT CARDS:** Visa, Mastercard, Amex, Diners

● **NOTES:**
Limited ♿ access to one floor, none to toilets.
Wine and snacks served 4pm-6pm, late-night snacks

● **DIRECTIONS:**
Ely Place runs off Merrion Row, which runs down from
St Stephen's Green, near to the Gallagher Gallery.

FRANK'S

Liz Mee & John Hayes
The Malting Tower
Grand Canal Quay,
Dublin 2
✆ **01-662 5870**
🖰 **www.franksbarandrestaurant.com**

You want to understand Dublin and its people? That's easy. Just have dinner in Frank's, and catch the city's pulse in this slick, vital city restaurant.

Before Liz Mee and John Hayes opened up Frank's, everyone told them it was in the wrong place.
Everyone was wrong.
Frank's, it seems, is at the centre of Dublin, or at least that is what it feels like on a busy night, which is just about every night. You want to take the pulse of this city and its people? Then you just need to have dinner and a few drinks in Frank's, and the mainline energy and motivation of Dublin will suddenly become apparent to you. Frank's is the zeitgeist, simple as that.
The cooking is simple and direct, thanks to Liz Mee's cool head and intellect, and also the fact that this kitchen does not have a head chef. Instead, it has a team, and that team fire out their trademark sandwiches – beef with bitter greens and caper vinaigrette – their eggs dishes – poached eggs with wild mushrooms and prosciutto – and the lovely mains. Regulars tend to order the specials that the kitchen has prepared, and finish with the affogato.

● **OPEN:** 11.30am-11pm Mon-Fri (bar closes 11.30pm); 12.30pm-11pm Sat-Sun (bar closes midnight Sat, 11pm Sun. Brunch served 12.30pm-5pm Sun)
● **PRICE:** Starters €7.50-€14.95 Mains €13.50-€32.95
● **CREDIT CARDS:** Visa, Mastercard, Amex, Laser

● **NOTES:**
♿ access.
Recommended for restaurant-loving children.

● **DIRECTIONS:**
Just over the canal bridge from Kitty O'Shea's pub.

L'GUEULETON

Declan O'Regan
1 Fade Street
Dublin 2
℅ **01-675 3708**

L'Gueuleton has been the success story of Dublin since opening, offering good food and good value.

L'Gueuleton has a simple, unfussy room with a neat little bar, an open kitchen and an electric ambience in which, wrote Elizabeth Field who used to mind a Dublin beat for Bridgestone central, "You observe that the crowd is tasting, sharing and engaging with their food. Sophistication-wise, you could be in any European capital."

That sophistication explains why L'G has been such a smash: we want sophistication, but we don't just want it on a Friday night, and we don't want to have to dress up for it and pay a skinful of money for it.

Troy Maguire's cooking is the key element of that sophistication, mainly because he doesn't do what everyone says he does: he doesn't cook French bistro food. He is smarter than that, taking French elements – haricots blancs with cod and mussels; Challans duck with sweetened chicory; roast pineapple with rum baba – but bending them to his own style. It's this creativity that provides the electricity, and which makes L'G such a wowee! hit.

● **OPEN:** 12.30pm-3pm, 6pm-10pm Mon-Sat
● **PRICE:** Lunch mains €11.50-€14.50, Dinner €30
● **CREDIT CARDS:** All major cards accepted

● **NOTES:**
♿ access. No reservations, although you can put your name down for a table if you call in after 6pm, and they will ring you back when it's ready.

● **DIRECTIONS:**
Fade St runs between Drury Street and South Great George's St. The restaurant is beside Hogan's Pub.

HO SEN

Tuan Nguyen & Tim Costigan
6 Cope Street
Dublin 2
☎ **01-671 8181**
🖰 **www.hosen.ie**

Ho Sen is the Temple Bar choice of hip, hard-working urban professionals who like to chill out with some Thai cooking. Oh, and we like it as well.

So there we are, Wednesday evening, Ho Sen, Temple Bar, having the crispy spring rolls, the rice paper rolls, the pancakes stuffed with pork and shrimp, the tofu with Vietnamese spices, the talapia in fish broth, the nice clean rice, the light beer, when it suddenly hits us that we are different.. Very different.

We are not twentysomething hard-working urban professionals. But tonight, Wednesday, everyone else in Ho Sen is. Everyone. Even the all-female waiting staff are twenty something hard-working urban professionals.

Now, don't imagine that this discomfited us an iota. It didn't. We are too old to be discomfited. But, it did show us that Ho Sen is hip, and that the sort of lean, crisp, clean Vietnamese cooking it offers is exactly what t-h-w-u-ps want at the end of a day spent fuelling the capitalist behemoth that is modern Dublin. Tim and Tuan seem to have gotten it just right, and service and value all chime with the cooking in being hip to the trip, and great, great fun.

● **OPEN:** noon-3pm Thur-Sun; 5pm-11pm Tue-Sun
● **PRICE:** Lunch €15, Dinner €20
● **CREDIT CARDS:** Visa, Mastercard, Laser

● **NOTES:**
No strict ♿ access, but staff would be happy to assist.

● **DIRECTIONS:**
Just behind the Central Bank in the Temple Bar district of Dublin city centre, south of the River Liffey.

JACOB'S LADDER

Adrian & Bernie Roche
4-5 Nassau Street
Dublin 2
© **01-670 3865**
🖨 **01-670 3868**
🖱 **www.jacobsladder.ie**

Adrian Roche's wildly imaginative cooking is a joy, producing some of the most original food in Dublin.

Whether or not you agree with the *Wall Street Journal* that Adrian Roche, chef-proprietor of Jacob's Ladder is "The most experimental chef in Dublin", what is unarguable about the cooking of this gifted individual is that it is quite unlike anyone else's work in the city. This culinary USP allies him with someone like Ben Gorman of The Mermaid Café. Mr Roche and Mr Gorman both take analytical, chess-master approaches to food, but their results are dramatically different.

Mr Roche's work does have a lot of experimental elements – a melon jelly with carpaccio of yellow fin tuna; almond foam with fillet of beef; an amazing dish where he pairs loin of lamb with goat's cheese, makes tortellini with braised lamb shank and finishes the dish with aubergine lamb jus – and if you crave this intelligent re-imagining of dishes, then nowhere is better than Jacob's Ladder. But it's not all lab science stuff: the rooms are comfy and lovely with great views, the service is ace, and value is superb.

● **OPEN:** 12.30pm-2.30pm, 6pm-10.30pm Tue-Fri; 12.30pm-2pm, 7pm-10pm Sat. Closed Sun & Mon, two weeks after Christmas, and early Aug.
● **PRICE:** Lunch €22-€29, Dinner €44-€75 (8-course)
● **CREDIT CARDS:** All major cards accepted

● **NOTES:**
Early Bird menu 6pm-7pm €21-€27.

● **DIRECTIONS:**
Upstairs on Nassau Street, over the vegetable shop, and overlooking Trinity College.

MACKEREL

Jay Bourke & Eoin Foyle
Bewley's Building
Grafton Street
Dublin 2
ⓒ **01-672 7719**
🖱 **www.mackerel.ie**

Bourke, Foyle and Walsh, saviours of Bewley's, creators of Mackerel, deserve the Freedom of Dublin city.

"There was a lump in my throat. I felt quite emotional. I didn't expect to. I just did. I don't know why. Perhaps I just thought: 'We had this unbelievable task, and we've done it: we've made it'. I was very emotional."

Jay Bourke, who with his partner Eoin Foyle and chef Eleanor Walsh has done the impossible, and made the old Bewley's on Grafton Street into a stonking success, confessed this to Shane Hegarty in *The Irish Times*. Bourke isn't alone. For all of us who watched as this great institution foundered during the 1990's, we all dreamt that Bewley's could be saved, that it could be made vital again, that it could, for heaven's sake, even become hip. Then you walk upstairs to Mackerel, and a hip crowd is enjoying Ms Walsh's lovely fish cooking, and a wave of emotion hits you. Saved, and just before the bell.

Mackerel is vital, and it sure is hip. Order the dishes of the day from the blackboard, order those very good Sicilian whites, and let the emotions sweep over you. Saved!

● **OPEN:** noon-4pm, 5pm-10pm Mon-Sun. Closed bank holidays.
● **PRICE:** Dinner €30
● **CREDIT CARDS:** All major cards accepted.

● **NOTES:**
♿ access.
Reservations recommended, especially at dinner.

● **DIRECTIONS:**
1st floor of Bewley's, on Grafton Street, which is Dublin's main shopping thoroughfare.

THE MERMAID CAFÉ

Ben Gorman & Mark Harrell
69/70 Dame Street
Temple Bar, Dublin 2
℡ **01-670 8236**
🖷 **01-670 8205**
🖱 **www.mermaid.ie**

The Mermaid is one of Dublin's great, original, punky restaurants, going strong after almost a decade.

Chef Temple Garner and front-of-house Ronan Ryan have departed The Mermaid to set up Town Bar & Grill, but Ben Gorman and Mark Harrell's brilliant, unorthodox Temple Bar restaurant remains as one of the great choices in Dublin. Some time back, our editor Orla Broderick put her finger right on the button when she wrote that "The food always manages to be fabulous, tasty, and yet different from anything else available in Dublin."

That difference is the Mermaid's USP – and, incidentally, it is as visible in their informal food bar, Gruel, right next door to the Mermaid. Ben Gorman seems to look at food in a fundamentally different way from most people. He take a very intellectual, analytical way with flavours, but he never gets trapped in the self-consciousness of molecular cooking or other sophistries. Instead, the food is sui generis: cod with confit onions, whiskey and mustard; cannelloni with Gorgonzola and sage; chicken with Parmesan polenta; Bailey's panna cotta. Thrilling food, great value.

● **OPEN:** 12.30pm-2.30pm, 6pm-11pm Mon-Sat; noon-3.30pm Sun brunch; 6pm-9pm Sun
● **PRICE:** Lunch €24, Dinner €40
● **CREDIT CARDS:** Visa, Mastercard, Amex, Laser

● **NOTES:**
♿ access. Reservations recommended.

● **DIRECTIONS:**
Dame Street runs from Trinity College up to Christchurch, and The Mermaid is half way up, beside the Olympia Theatre.

MINT

Patricia Courtney
47 Ranelagh Village
Dublin 6
© **01-497 8655**
🖰 **www.mintrestaurant.ie**

Oliver Dunne is right on
top of his game right now,
making Mint the don't-miss
destination for hot cooking.

Oliver Dunne is right on top of his game these days, and
his inspired cooking has served to make Mint one of the
hottest destinations in Dublin, at the same time as winning this young man the admiration of his professional
peers. When the hot chefs of Ireland are calling you the
hot chef, then you are truly firing on all cylinders, and that
is right where Mint and Mr Dunne are at.
He likes the light, ethereal elements that are so popular
amongst chefs in the post-Ferran Adria world – the foams
made with mushrooms, the cappucinos made with shellfish and alcohol. But there is a very rustic beat to this
chef's style – he will cook Clonakilty black pudding with
his scallops and unify them with a fish jus, or he will manage to make a goat's cheese panna cotta work (most people can't), and serve it with pickled onion. For the thrill of
sheer wild creativity, Mint can't be beat right now, and if
it's tricky to get a table, becaue of the very limited seat-
ing capacity, then just keep on trying.

- **OPEN:** 6pm-10pm Tue-Sun; noon-3pm Fri & Sun.
- **PRICE:** Lunch €23.50-€29.50, Dinner €45,
- **CREDIT CARDS:** Visa, Mastercard, Amex,

- **NOTES:**
♿ access.
Pre-theatre menu €28-€35.

- **DIRECTIONS:**
Mint is opposite the 24 hour Spar, and Appian Way, next
to the Kelli boutique, and right smack in the centre of
Ranelagh village.

MONTY'S OF KATHMANDU

Shiva Gautam
28 Eustace St, Temple Bar
Dublin 2
℡ **01-670 4911**
🖨 **01-494 4359**
🖰 **www.montys.ie**

Monty's of Kathmandu is a Temple Bar restaurant that mercifully isn't a tourist trap, serving the most delicious Nepalese cooking to hungry locals.

Shiva Gautam is an ambitious, focused, determined individual, and all of his dynamic energy is channelled into making Monty's the very best that it can be. With a very simple and unpretentious Temple Bar room to work with, and a crack team in the kitchen, Mr Gautam has made Monty's into one of the key Temple Bar destinations, and a beacon of true ethnic cooking in a sea of otherwise indifferent restaurants.

The food is Nepalese in origin, which makes it sufficiently familiar for some, and engagingly different for others. If we had a recommendation, it would be to lean towards their superb tandoori dishes, for there is masterly skill with the tandoor in this restaurant, shown both in the tandoor dishes and in their amazing breads. But, to be honest, we have never had anything less than splendid food every time we have eaten here, and the consistency and creativity is as gratifying as the bright, vivid flavours. Great food, great value, and everyone acts like a regular.

● **OPEN:** noon-2.30pm, 6pm-11.30pm Mon-Sat; 6pm-11pm Sun
● **PRICE:** Meals €25-€30
● **CREDIT CARDS:** Visa, Mastercard, Amex, Laser

● **NOTES:**
♿ access, but not to toilets.

● **DIRECTIONS:**
Opposite the film centre in the Temple Bar area, which is adjacent to the River Liffey, running between Dame Street and the river.

NOSH

Sacha & Samantha Farrell
111 Coliemore Road
Dalkey
County Dublin
☎ **01-284 0666**
🖰 **www.nosh.ie**

Samantha and Sacha Farrell's local culinary heroine, Nosh, is a classy room with classy, direct cooking, great service and great value for money.

"Great room, brilliant service, just the sort of relaxed, welcoming space that appeals to all ages – simply excellent."

Well, we did have a jolly old evening last time we were in Nosh, didn't we, at least according to our notes? Mind you, we weren't alone. Everyone seemed to be having a great old time, happy to be in out of the rain, happy to have the smells and scents of Nosh lapping you into a little oasis of luxury. Samantha and Sacha aren't trying to re-invent the wheel in Nosh. Instead, they are focused on doing what they do as well as they can do it, and doing it consistently, modestly, and meaningfully. No egos, then, just good service, a great room, and lovely grub: excellent goat's cheese fritters to begin, a classy, punchy, invigorating starter, then lemon sole with crabmeat and mash, just to show that they can do the comfort food with accuracy, and then a crème brûlée delivered as a Crème brulée should be. No rocket science, so, just precision cooking.

● **OPEN:** noon-4pm, 6pm-late Tue-Sun (brunch served Sat & Sun)
● **PRICE:** Lunch €13, Dinner €32
● **CREDIT CARDS:** Visa, Mastercard

● **NOTES:**
♿ access. Early Bird menu Tue-Fri, 6pm-7.45pm, €19 for 2 courses, €21 for 3 courses

● **DIRECTIONS:**
The restaurant is just off the main street of the village as you turn left: it's on the right and and easy to find.

O'CONNELL'S

Tom O'Connell
@ Bewley's Hotel, Merrion Rd
Ballsbridge, Dublin 4
℡ **01-647 3304**
🖷 **01-647 3398**
🖱 **www.oconnellsballsbridge.com**

Tom O'Connell's brilliant
restaurant manages to give
customers what they want
just the way they want it.

There is no more adept student of the restaurant business than Tom O'Connell, which means that there is no restaurant more adept at giving the customer what they want than O'Connell's. Working a stage in O'Connell's ought to be a rite of passage for everyone in the restaurant business, for working with Mr O'Connell would teach everyone how to respond to the ever-changing needs of customers.

What it would also teach students is that certain things never change – people want value, service, and food that is properly sourced and cooked with flair. O'Connell's delivers: Kilmore Quay whiting with mint and pea purée; Hickey's farm duck with buttered cabbage; organic loin of pork with mustard sauce. Many of the dishes can be ordered as small courses, a trend Mr O'Connell has noted that many diners now prefer, and the menu is predominantly gluten-free, with many dishes for coeliacs. Value for money is the best in the city, and O'C's rocks.

● **OPEN:** 7am-10.30am (breakfast), 12.30pm-2.30pm (buffet menu), 2.30pm-6pm (afternoon menu, table service), 6pm-10pm (dinner) Mon-Sun
● **PRICE:** Lunch €10-85-€12.85, Set dinner €27.50
● **CREDIT CARDS:** All major cards accepted.

● **NOTES:**
Full wheelchair access.

● **DIRECTIONS:**
Basement of Bewley's Hotel on Merrion Rd, round the corner from the RDS.

ONE PICO

Eamonn O'Reilly
5-6 Molesworth Place
Schoolhouse Lane, Dublin 2
✆ **01-676 0300**
🖷 **01-676 0411**
🖰 **www.onepico.com**

Eamonn O'Reilly mines his own vein
of contemporary Irish and European
cookery, adding in nice grace notes to
many classic culinary combinations.

Eamonn O'Reilly is really a classic cook at heart, though
he has a reputation as an experimenter, even as a guy who
used to dabble a little in the minefield that is the complex
and confusing world of molecular cooking.

But when you look at his menus, and you eat his cooking,
you see someone who is pretty firmly in the tradition –
scallops come with boudin noir, as you might expect, ray
wing has a beurre noisette, duck confit has red cabbage
beef fillet comes with pommes Anna. But O'Reilly now
likes to work his variations on these classics, making that
beurre noisette with sultanas, adding beetroot into that
red cabbage, putting fig chutney and sauce Jacqueline with
the scallops and the boudin noir, adding an unexpected
tarragon essence with the beef fillet. It all makes for satisfying and challenging eating, and the crew at One Pico
make it work, and the only quibble one tends to hear is
about the size of portions. Prices are keen for this level
of cooking, and the room is extremely handsome.

● **OPEN:** 12.30pm-2.30pm, 6pm-10.30pm Mon-Sat.
Closed bank holidays & first two weeks in August.
● **PRICE:** Lunch €25, Dinner €50-€60
● **CREDIT CARDS:** Visa, Mastercard, Amex

● **NOTES:**
Limited ♿ access. Reservations recommended.
Pre-theatre menu €35, 6pm-7pm.

● **DIRECTIONS:**
On the corner of a small laneway – Molesworth Place –
which runs between Dawson Street and Kildare Street.

101 TALBOT

Margaret Duffy & Pascal Bradley
101 Talbot Street
Dublin 1
✆ **01-874 5011**
🖨 **01-875 5011**
🖱 **www.101talbot.com**

The writer Frank Corr wrote that the secret of 101 Talbot is that it is as much club, as restaurant. Everyone who eats here behaves like a member.

"It is as much club as restaurant", is how the gastronomic writer Frank Corr once described 101 Talbot, one of Dublin city's landmark restaurants. Mr Corr is right, and yet what is curious is that the clubby designation applies to the sense of ownership that regular customers have for this great restaurant, but does not apply in any way to any sense of exclusivity: 101 is a club for all who discover its wacky, wayward charms, and as a destination it has always worked as the antithesis of snobbery.

Pascal and Margaret have always run the most democratic place in the city, and you will find all manner of odds and sods here; people who relish the unique Dublin spirit and energy that is the 101 characteristic. Of course, the punters also love the food, with its Mediterranean borrowings, its strong vegetarian focus, its lightness of touch and tasty honesty, and they love the friendly service and hip attitude of the funky staff. Only Pascal and Margaret could have created a club for everyone: no mean feat.

● **OPEN:** 5pm-11pm Tue-Sat
● **PRICE:** Dinner €30
● **CREDIT CARDS:** Visa, Mastercard, Amex, Laser, Maestro

● **NOTES:**
Reservations recommended at weekends.
Recommended for vegetarians.

● **DIRECTIONS:**
3 minutes' walk from the Dublin Spire, in the direction of Connolly Station, upstairs, on the right-hand side.

ROLY'S BISTRO

Colin O'Daly
7 Ballsbridge Terrace
Ballsbridge, Dublin 4
℡ **01-668 2611**
📠 **01-660 8535**
🖱 **www.rolysbistro.com**

Colin O'Daly's rollicking Roly's is one of Dublin's culinary institutions, and if it's a grande dame at this stage, it still has the vital energy of a young pup.

Back in 1993, when Roly's made its debut in the Bridgestone 100 Best Restaurants, the Dublin restaurant world included The Kapriol, Le Coq Hardi, Roberto Pons cooking in Il Ristorante in Dalkey, Vincent Vis cooking in The Gastrognome and the late Eddie Bates cooking in the Irish Film Centre. Even amidst such distinguished company, however, Roly's made a huge impact on the city, an impact that continues a dozen years down the line.

Colin O'Daly and head chef Paul Cartwright could coast along with their signature dishes – beef with green peppercorns; roast lamb with juniper berries; game pie with cranberry; Kerry lamb pie; chocolate truffle tart, to name check just a few of a very long list – but the competition from every new kid on the block has meant that they stay keen and focused, giving this explosively lively big brasserie just the right sort of motivation to keep it on top. Sometimes Roly's can get a little too clamorous and busy, but we kind of like it like that.

- **OPEN:** noon-3pm, 6pm-10pm Mon-Sun
- **PRICE:** Lunch €20, Dinner €40-€50
- **CREDIT CARDS:** All major cards accepted

- **NOTES:**
♿ access. Early Bird 3-courses, 6pm-6.45pm Mon-Thur €24

- **DIRECTIONS:**
On the corner of Ballsbridge and Herbert Park, where all the traffic lights occur at the top of Shelbourne Road, just between the American Embassy and the RDS.

THORNTON'S

Kevin & Muriel Thornton
St. Stephen's Green
Dublin 2
☎ **01-478 7008**
🖷 **01-478 7009**
🖰 **www.thorntonsrestaurant.com**

No other chef cooks like
Kevin Thornton, a cook
whose signature style is
unique and transcendent.

Everyone has so many opinions about Kevin Thornton's
restaurant – about the prices, the ambience, the formality,
blah, blah blah – that we are in danger of losing sight of
the fundamental truth about this exemplary chef.
That truth is that Kevin Thornton's style is utterly,
recognisably, his own, and there are few cooks about
whom one can truly say that. Whatever you eat here,
from mallard glazed with honey and pistachio to trio of
blue fin tuna, to seabass with white truffle risotto to
pheasant with shallot tatin to his classic pears with red
wine and vanilla, it will be cooked as no other chef would
cook the dish. Thornton, therefore, has transcended his
influences and his education, and achieved a rare state of
unique creativity where everything is signed with his
signature. Most importantly, that signature is not just
Thornton, it is Thornton's Irish Cooking, a meld of the
classic and the contemporary with a very Irish
robustness. So, ignore the debate, and focus on the food.

● **OPEN:** 12.30pm-2pm, 7pm-10.30pm Tue-Sat
● **PRICE:** Lunch €30-€40, Dinner €95-€120
● **CREDIT CARDS:** All major cards accepted

● **NOTES:**
Full wheelchair access.
Recommended for vegetarians.

● **DIRECTIONS:**
In the centre of Dublin, on the west side of St Stephen's
Green. The restaurant has an entrance at the side of the
Fitzwilliam Hotel.

10 RESTAURANTS
WITH GREAT VALUE

1

BROCKA ON THE WATER
BALLINDERRY, CO TIPPERARY

2

CROCKET'S ON THE QUAY
BALLINA, Co MAYO

3

GINGER
BELFAST, Co ANTRIM

4

GRANGECON CAFÉ
BLESSINGTON, Co WICKLOW

5

L'GUEULETON
DUBLIN, Co DUBLIN

6

LA MARINE
ROSSLARE, Co WEXFORD

7

THE MILL
DUNFANAGHY, CO DONEGAL

8

NUREMORE HOTEL
CARRICKMACROSS, Co MONAGHAN

9

OUT OF THE BLUE
DINGLE, Co KERRY

10

THE TANNERY
DUNGARVAN, Co WATERFORD

TOWN BAR & GRILL

Temple Garner & Ronan Ryan
21 Kildare St
Dublin 2
© **01- 662 4724**
🖰 **www.townbarandgrill.com**

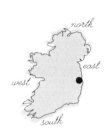

Temple Garner and Ronan
Ryan have made Town
B&G into one of the three
hottest tickets in town.

The basement space of Town B&G has had more occupants over the last few years than most chefs have had hot dinners. But Temple Garner and Ronan Ryan have changed all that, and today Town battles it out with Mint and L'Geueleton as to who is the hottest ticket in Dublin. Garner and Ryan moved up town after working together in the iconic Mermaid Café. so they have chutzpah and confidence aplenty, something that made early service glitches all the more surprising.

But what was rock-steady from day one was savoury cooking with sheer power. The influence on the food is Italian, but the power seems to us to be undiluted Spanish-style machismo, which means you should order the meat courses: milk-fed veal with white beans and artichokes; slow-roast lamb shank with basil and aubergine Campania; rib-eye steak with sage and mustard mash, for these are grandstanding dishes that demand big Italian red wines, and a late night. Hot stuff.

● **OPEN:** noon-11pm Mon-Sat; 5pm-10pm Sun
● **PRICE:** Dinner €40, House wine €25
● **CREDIT CARDS:** Visa, Mastercard, Amex

● **NOTES:**
No wheelchair access.
Health-conscious low-sodium kid's menu. Live jazz on Sundays.

● **DIRECTIONS:**
In the basement of Mitchell's Wine Cellars, opposite the side of the Shelburne Hotel, just off Stephen's Green.

ARD BIA

Aoibheann McNamara
2 Quay Street, Galway
County Galway
℡ **091-539 897**
🖰 **www.ardbia.com**

Café, restaurant, art space and lots more besides, Ard Bia is a busy, bustling restaurant and recreation space that is a key Galway spot.

Exhibition space. Cookery classes. Wine dinners. Art happenings. With all that is going on in Ard Bia, apart from its café and restaurant, it's a wonder that anyone has time to cook dinner but, thankfully, Aoibheann McNamara's pretty, funky space upstairs on Quay Street does get around to rattling the pots and pans, and does so with some style.

The menu lays out the dish contents very directly – Gubbeen Plate: salami, smoked bacon; cheese; 10oz sirloin steak, pommes frites, black pepper sauce, roasted tomato; though when the roast Donegal cod can boast a "virgin sauce" you suspect that things in Ard Bia may not always be entirely straightforward, but we were too shy and giggly to ask just exactly how a "virgin sauce" is made. What is most important about Ard Bia, however, is that it captures the spirit of Galway in its feisty, somewhat over-ambitious innocence and, as such, it is a major asset to a city that has few good, creative, distinctive eateries.

● **OPEN:** Café open 10am-5pm Mon-Sat; noon-6pm Sun. Restaurant open 6.30pm-10.30pm
● **PRICE:** Cafe lunch €10-€12, Dinner €34
● **CREDIT CARDS:** Visa, Mastercard, Laser

● **NOTES:**
Cookery classes promoting healthy cooking take place in autumn and spring. Art Gallery.

● **DIRECTIONS:**
Quay Street is the central street of Galway. Note that it is pedestrianised.

BALLYNAHINCH CASTLE

Patrick O'Flaherty
Ballinafad, Recess
County Galway
℡ **095-31006**
🖷 **095-31085**
🖰 **www.ballynahinch-castle.com**

Never mind fashionable
Dublin city restaurants:
Ballynahinch Castle is the
hardest place to get a table.

Dubliners love to talk about which capital city restaurant is the hottest ticket, and which is the most difficult table to get access to.

The answer is Ballynahinch. Which is, of course, at the opposite side of the country to Dublin. Sorry about that. To put things into context, we last tried to get a table in the bar – not even the restaurant – arguing that if we came with the family at 5.30pm we would be gone by 7pm. They couldn't accommodate us. How has this happened? How is the hottest ticket a big pile of a castle in the middle of Connemara? The answer is that Ballynahinch is run by a dream team, led by manager Patrick O'Flaherty and chef Robert Webster. It is a joy to see this crew at work, happy in their creative dynamic, and firing out fantastic food – duck confit en croûte; sautéed rabbit with artichokes; duck breast with buttered summer vegetables; wild salmon with savoy cabbage – modest, balanced cooking that suits the light, pretty room.

- **OPEN:** 6.30pm-9pm Mon-Sun
- **PRICE:** Dinner €49 + 10% service charge
- **CREDIT CARDS:** All major cards accepted.

- **NOTES:**
Wheelchair access to restaurant only. Great food served in the bar. Reservations essential in both restaurant and bar.

- **DIRECTIONS:**
6.5km after Recess on the N59 towards Clifden, turn left on road signposted for Roundstone & Ballynahinch.

NIMMO'S

Dave Sweeney
Spanish Arch
Galway
County Galway
℅ **091-561114**

Harriet Leander has stepped down from Nimmo's, whilst Dave Sweeney has taken over. But, nothing will change, all will stay as is. Hooray!

Harriet Leander has stepped down from the day-to-day mania of the magnificent Nimmo's, and Dave Sweeney has taken up the reins, so now is the right time to let us praise famous women. Ms Leander, right from the days when Nimmo's was firstly known as The Blue Raincoat - and where cheese mogul Seamus Sheridan first rattled the pans — and then throughout the history of Nimmo's in the 1990's and later, ran the restaurant that defined Galway. Nimmo's was wild, busy, crazy, fun, loud, boisterous, and its mix of Mediterranean-style food and super wines, served by one of the best teams in the country, was simply irresistible. In a city where standards of food are often low, Ms Leander kept standards high, and her achievement was an altogether mighty one. Mr Sweeney is doing nothing new, save for a little jazz on Monday nights. "It works, and it is, so we have just carried on", says Mr Sweeney. Good news for Galway, then, and good news for the west coast, good news for food lovers.

- **OPEN:** 6pm-10pm Tue-Sun; 1pm-3pm Fri-Sat
- **PRICE:** Lunch €4.50-€17.50, Dinner €35-€40
- **CREDIT CARDS:** Visa, Mastercard, Laser

- **NOTES:**
♿ access access (though happy to help).
Not recommended for children.

- **DIRECTIONS:**
The old stone building directly underneath the Spanish Arch, across from the Jury's Hotel.

THE OLD SCHOOLHOUSE

Kenneth Connolly
Clarinbridge
County Galway
✆ **091-796898**
🖨 **091-796117**
🖰 **kenc@iol.ie**

The Old Schoolhouse is a restaurant where great personal care is taken over every detail of the cooking, the service and presentation of the food.

It tells you a great deal about the care he takes with sourcing supplies, that Kenneth Connolly brings all his meats for the Old Schoolhouse all the way from James McGeough's butchers, which means all the way from Oughterard in Connemara. There are restaurants in Connemara that are foolish enough not to source from McGeough's, but then, they aren't in the 100 best restaurants, and the Old Schoolhouse is.

Mr Connolly is also not above getting vegetables from his dad's garden to add flourish to menus in TOS, and this personal, principled application shines through in some lovely food – trio of organic Aran island smoked salmon; McGeough's lamb sausage with rosemary polenta; brochette of monkfish with mango and coriander; rhubarb and apple crumble. This is approachable, enjoyable food, cooked and served with optimum professionalism, and that professionalism explains why locals from Clarinbridge and Oranmore pack out TOS.

● **OPEN:** 6.30pm-10pm Tue-Sun; 12.30pm-2.30pm Sun
● **PRICE:** Lunch €22, Dinner €32
● **CREDIT CARDS:** Visa, Mastercard, Amex

● **NOTES:**
Wheelchair access.
Children's menu €10

● **DIRECTIONS:**
On the Galway-Limerick Road, 11km from Galway city, in the centre of Clarinbridge. Signposted.

PANGUR BÁN

John Walsh & Mairead Tucker
Letterfrack
Connemara,
County Galway
© 095) 41243
www.pangurban.com

John and Mairead Walsh's Pangur Bán restaurant is the got-to-get-there address in Connemara for real food, served in a traditional cottage.

John Walsh is a very imaginative cook. Few are the Irish chefs who would put spicy black beans with a sirloin steak, or who would cook wild pigeon in cider and cream (isn't cider and cream for pork?), or who will braise organic lamb shank in ale, and he really likes to push the boat out with things like smoked wild boar sausage with butterbeans and sun-dried tomatoes, or hake baked with brie, or tuna with horseradish mash, or wild venison in a stew with Guinness and shiitake mushrooms, all challenging and provocative pairings.

This iconoclastic approach makes for fun eating, in a charming restaurant with a very special old-cottage style and ambience, and some excellent paintings. Above all, Pangur Bán is pivotal as a creative restaurant in an area with precious few good eating destinations, and the polish of the service only serves to confirm its special status. Prices are also very fair, with many main courses well under twenty euro, so food and value in PB are spot on.

● **OPEN:** 6pm-9pm, Mon-Sun high-season Tue-Sun; mid-season Wed-Sun low-season. Closed Oct-Xmas, Jan & Feb
● **PRICE:** Dinner €32
● **CREDIT CARDS:** Visa, Mastercard, Laser

● **NOTES:**
Full disabled access. Always telephone off season.
Cookery classes Mar-April

● **DIRECTIONS:**
Letterfrack is 14.5km from Clifden on the Westport road. Restaurant is opposite Connemara National Park.

DA ROBERTA

**Sandro and Roberta Pieri
169 Upper Salthill
Galway, County Galway
℮ 091-585 808
🖳 091-583 455
⌃ daroberta@eircom.net**

Simple Italian food cooked with care, and a great, spirited ambience, means that everyone loves Sandro and Roberta's restaurant in Salthill.

Visitors to Galway tend to damn Da Roberta with faint praise, suggesting that if it was in any other Irish city, it wouldn't rate serious scrutiny, and that it is only because destination addresses in Galway are so scarce that it gets attention from guidebooks and writers.

This is unfair. Da Roberta is a success thanks to correct and unpretentious Italian cooking, the sort of thing that everywhere else gets all wrong, but which Sandro and Roberta get spot on. The breads are good. The pizzas are good. The pastas are only excellent. They cook from instinct and intuition, rather than succumbing to the red sauce cliché that is evident everywhere else, so there is an ever-appealing freshness and acuity about the cooking: it may be Italian classics writ large, but there is nothing wrong with that in our book, when the dishes are cooked and served with the amiable perspicacity you find in this clubbable room. The right room, the right food, the right place, the right price. And the cynics are quite wrong.

- **OPEN:** noon-11pm Mon-Sun
- **PRICE:** Meals €12-€30
- **CREDIT CARDS:** Visa, Mastercard, Amex, Maestro

- **NOTES:**
No wheelchair access.

- **DIRECTIONS:**
Salthill is on the other side of the main bridge in Galway city centre - so drive over the River Corrib, following signs for Salthill, and the restaurant is opposite the church in Salthill.

SLATEFORT RESTAURANT

Maura & Rosario Winters
Slatefort, Bullaun
Loughrea, County Galway
℡ **091-870 667**
🖷 **091-870 667**
🖰 **slateforthouse@eircom.net**

Rather remote and off-the-beaten-track, Slatefort is the surprising place to find real Italian cooking from Maura and Rosario Winters.

Maura Winters has taken up the kitchen reins at Slatefort – which has also now dropped the "House" from its name, as Mrs Winters was concerned that some folk might have thought this modest restaurant was in some way a "posh" house. The Italian theme, and the Italian-named dishes, that has characterised the cooking from their opening, continues apace, with the majority of the dishes continuing to be themes and variations on the dishes cooked by the previous Italian chefs: pan-fried squid stuffed with prawns; aubergine and mozzarella baked with tomato sauce; seabass baked in salt; cod with tomatoes and olives; spaghetti with tuna, olives and cherry tomatoes' chicken wrapped in Parma ham with soft cheese stuffing. Mrs Winters is an inquisitive, modest cook, which suits this light, precise style of Italian cooking, giving it a real casalingua style, though some may regret that the choices now are more conservative than before. But this is a cook and a restaurant to keep a close eye on.

● **OPEN:** 6.30pm-11pm Tue- Sun; 1pm-3pm Sun. Closed Mon-Wed off season.
● **PRICE:** Dinner €34, Sun lunch €20
● **CREDIT CARDS:** Visa, Mastercard, Amex, Diners

● **NOTES:**
Wheelchair access.

● **DIRECTIONS:**
New road to Bullaun opening late 2005 - From the Galway to Dublin road, leave at the second roundabout and follow signs for Bullaun & New Inn.

ALLO'S BAR & BISTRO

Helen Mullane
41 Church Street
Listowel
County Kerry
✆ **068-22880**
🖷 **068-22803**

The archetypal Irish gastro pub, Allo's was cooking creative food and serving it with style, in this lovely bar, years before anyone else dreamed about it.

Tempura of plaice with garlic roast potatoes and salad. Spicy potato wedges and chicken wings. Tikka chicken with basmati rice and raita.

It doesn't sound like much, does it? The roll-call of what the McKenna tribe had to eat at lunchtime in Allo's on our last flying visit through north Kerry after getting off the ferry at Tarbert. It sounds like bar food, the sort of thing you might eat anywhere and, if Allo's is a bar, doesn't that make this bar food? Well, yes Allo's is a bar – one of very few whose bricolage style we actually like – and the food is simple. But, the point about Allo's is that the food is devastatingly delicious, thanks to using superb ingredients, and thanks to Armel Whyte and his team of Theo and Gerry in the kitchen firing out food that is drop-dead delicious. Helen Mullane keeps front of house in tip-top shape, and there are even some excellent rooms should you decide to have dinner and stay late. They make it all look so simple, but it is not simple at all.

- **OPEN:** Noon-9.15pm Tue-Sat
- **PRICE:** Lunch €10-€16, Dinner €50
- **CREDIT CARDS:** Visa, Mastercard, Amex

- **NOTES:**
Reservations recommended. Wheelchair access.

- **DIRECTIONS:**
1 hour's drive from Limerick on the N69. Allo's is in the centre of Listowel, opposite the Garda station. Follow the one-way system and keep turning to the right and you will wind up at Allo's, on the left of Church Street.

THE CHART HOUSE

Jim & Carmel McCarthy
The Mall, Dingle
County Kerry
✆ **066-915 2255**
🖷 **095-915 2255**
🖰 **www.charthousedingle.com**

With chef Noel Enright re-energising the Chart House kitchen crew, this busy restaurant has never been in better form, with ace food and wines.

With Noel Enright heading up an ace kitchen crew, Jim and Carmel McCarthy's Chart House has been on a rollercoaster ride all year long, producing great cooking and opening great wines for droves of happy punters.

Mr Enright has given a new charge and focus to the signature dishes of the Chart House, making these great comfort creations even more attractive – the superb local Annascaul black pudding in filo pastry with apple chutney: the spiced chicken sausage with hot pepper marmalade; the roast Kerry lamb with red onion and feta tarte tatin; the roast guinea fowl with red cabbage; the peppered pork with brandied apricots.

But what sets the Chart House apart is the success of its total experience; the room, the atmosphere, the service, the food, the wines and the value are all of a piece. You are happy the moment you walk in this room, and you are happy until you leave. That's why you might have read about them in *Vanity Fair*, or *Forbes*, or the Bridgestones.

● **OPEN:** 6.30pm-10pm Mon-Sun (closed Mon & Tue off season, and restaurant closes 7 Jan-Valentine's Day)
● **PRICE:** Dinner €38
● **CREDIT CARDS:** Visa, Mastercard, Laser

● **NOTES:**
♿ access. Value menu, dinner €35
Importing a selection of South African wines.

● **DIRECTIONS:**
Directly at the roundabout, on the left-hand side, as you approach Dingle from the Killarney direction.

GABY'S

Gert & Marie Maes
27 High Street, Killarney
County Kerry
✆ **064-32519**
🖨 **064-32747**
🖱 **www.gabysireland.com**

Vividly efficient, and a perennial destination in Killarney town, Gert and Marie Maes' ultra-professional Gaby's restaurant is a pure charmer.

You could walk in the door of Gaby's on a busy summer's night, take a look at all the over-tanned golfers in luridly coloured sweaters quaffing rare American wines, glance at the menu with its translations of dishes into German, French and Dutch, look at the somewhat dated design style of the restaurant, and think: "This is a tourist trap! get me out of here!"

Steady on. Gert and Marie Maes and their crew haven't prospered for a couple of decades by selling rubbish to tourists with too much money and too little taste. Gaby's is a super-professional restaurant, and the cooking is real and committed, and much more up-to-the-minute than the room, which explains why it works and continues to work. Gert Maes is a hungry chef, who knows all the contemporary trends, and it is this precision that keeps the fish and shellfish cookery in Gaby's right up to the bar. So, focus on the fish and shellfish cookery, leave the pricey bottles to the golfers, and you will have a ball in Gaby's.

● **OPEN:** 6pm-10pm Mon-Sat
● **PRICE:** Dinner €50
● **CREDIT CARDS:** All major cards accepted.

● **NOTES:**
Wheelchair access with assistance.
Closed Christmas and mid Feb-mid Mar.

● **DIRECTIONS:**
In the centre of Killarney, just down from the market cross. Look out for their famous sign of three fishermen underneath a Curragh.

THE KILLARNEY PARK HOTEL

Odran Lucey
Kenmare Place
Killarney, County Kerry
✆ **064-35555**
📠 **064-35266**
🖰 **www.killarneyparkhotel.ie**

Great cooking in The Park restaurant, and great food in the bar, makes the KP an unmissable address.

When people write about the cooking in the KP they rightly focus on the superb cooking of their glam Park Restaurant. But, that isn't the only great cooking you will find here, for the food served in the bar of the KP is also superb, and it is served with an attention to detail that is unmatched anywhere else in the town. That attention alone explains why the people of Killarney eat here – they want the mushy peas served with battered fish and chips to be that good, they want the tartare sauce with lemon sole to be just right, and they know that they will get that precision every time.

So, don't miss the bar food, and don't miss The Park, for this is cooking as it should be in every great hotel dining room: rich but restrained, expert yet not fussy, and hugely enjoyable and served with panache. We'll have the oysters with a shot of bloody mary, then venison with roast parsnips and smoked aubergine, then summer pudding, and we will relish this true, creative, masterly Irish food.

- **OPEN:** 7.30am-10am, 7pm-9pm Mon-Sun
- **PRICE:** Dinner €60
- **CREDIT CARDS:** Visa, Mastercard, Amex, Laser

- **NOTES:**
♿ access. Bar food served daily. Children welcome.

- **DIRECTIONS:**
Centre of Killarney. At 1st roundabout (travelling from Cork) take the 1st exit for town centre.
At 2nd roundabout take 2nd exit, at 3rd take 1st, the hotel is on the left.

MULCAHY'S

Bruce Mulcahy
36 Henry Street
Kenmare
County Kerry
℅ **064-42383**

Bruce Mulcahy can cook anything and everything, and do it all with style and creative accomplishment.

Bruce Mulcahy's elegant and light-filled room in the heart of Kenmare is a glam setting for one of the most quixotic and accomplished cooks working today. Mr Mulcahy's USP is simple; he can cook everything, and do so with authority and satisfying veracity and accuracy. His menus range from sushi and sashimi to duck confit with sweet potato gratin to lamb shank ravioli with red wine sauce, and everything is delivered with polish and imagination. What's more, he can pull off a dinner of scallops with tempura of cauliflower to those superb lamb shank ravioli to classy lemon tart with a fantastic milk and almond ice cream, and he won't put a foot wrong, or have an element out of place. This seamless professionalism is a thrill, and Mr Mulcahy pulls all the elements together: great service, great sounds, smart room, and they do lovely foods for children, which shows their generosity and care. Mulcahy's defines the creativity of the contemporary Irish dining experience in the best way, and it's a happening place.

● **OPEN:** 6pm-10pm Mon-Sun (closed Tue & Wed off-season)
● **PRICE:** Dinner €38-€40
● **CREDIT CARDS:** All major cards accepted.

● **NOTES:**
♿ access.

● **DIRECTIONS:**
In the centre of Kenmare, on the right-hand side as you travel down the one-way street, coming from Glengarriff.

OUT OF THE BLUE

Tim Mason
Waterside
Dingle
County Kerry
℗ **066-915 0811**
✒ **ootb@eircom.net**

Tim Mason's OOTB
marries ambition with
achievement to create one
of the best fish restaurants.

"Sometimes we really do need a bigger place, but I am loath to do that, and lose what we might have", says Tim Mason of his small, perfectly formed and absolutely cult Dingle destination, Out of the Blue. Forget that "what we mighty have" modesty: what OotB does have – and no mights about it – is the best fish, the best wines, the best fun. It is an archetypal restaurant, just as Fishy Fishy or Good Things or Café Hans are archetypes: they are places that satisfy our imagination, our primal wishes, just as much as our appetites. As you drive into Dingle, your head is saying: "I would love a little seafront place with monkfish with prawn parmentier, or grilled lobster, or crab claws in garlic butter, and a glass of Chablis – and then, there it is: Out of the Blue. And inside there is a little bar, and the wine list is superb, and the fun is mighty, and your archetypal wishes are satisfied. Mr Mason speaks of trying to achieve "an interested, happy and hard-working place". That is just what OotB is: ambition achieved.

● **OPEN:** 12.30pm-3pm, 6.30pm-9.30pm Mon-Sat; 6pm-8pm Sun. Open every day except Wed. Closed Nov-Feb
● **PRICE:** Lunch €14-€18, Dinner €30-€40
● **CREDIT CARDS:** Visa, Mastercard

● **NOTES:**
♿ access to front table in shop. Wine Bar now open. Restaurant closes if they run out of fish. Crayfish a speciality.

● **DIRECTIONS:**
Directly opposite the main pier in Dingle.

PACKIE'S

Martin Hallissey
Henry Street
Kenmare
County Kerry
✆ **064-41508**
🖷 **064-42135**

Packie's is one the great
Irish restaurants, with
sublime comfort food from
owner Martin Hallissey.

Martin Hallissey is the sort of cook who cooks dishes you would be happy to spend the rest of your life eating. Seafood sausage with beurre blanc. Confit duck leg with caramelised pear and ginger. Baked cod provençale style. Dover sole meunière. Crumbed scallops with lemon. Roast chicken with glazed shallots and tarragon gravy. Traditional lamb stew with fresh herbs. Coffee parfait with whiskey cream.

Are your lips smacking? Doesn't the simple act of reading those dishes summon up ravenous hunger pangs? That is this man's brilliance, and the brilliance of his cooking: even before you get into the cosy space of Packie's, you are salivating at the prospect. So, bring on the wild sea bass with red pepper relish, let's have the rack of lamb with lentilles de Puy, and then a little pot of chocolate, and something nice to drink. Throughout its long history, Packie's has been a life-affirming restaurant experience, and today Mr Hallissey carries on that tradition, grandly.

● **OPEN:** 6pm-10pm Mon-Sat. Weekends only Nov-Dec. Open one week before Christmas. Closed New Year-St Patrick's Day weekend.
● **PRICE:** Dinner €45
● **CREDIT CARDS:** Visa, Mastercard

● **NOTES:**
♿ access. (but not to toilets).

● **DIRECTIONS:**
In the centre of Kenmare, on the right, the first street you meet when coming into the town from Glengarriff.

THE BALLYMORE INN

Georgina & Barry O'Sullivan
Ballymore Eustace
County Kildare
℡ **045-864 585**
🖷 **045-864 747**
🖑 **theballymoreinn@eircom.net**

Every detail of every dish
on the Ballymore's menus
is blessed with utmost care
from Georgina O'Sullivan.

A planned, large-scale building project has proven to be a
slow builder in Georgina and Barry O'Sullivan's iconic
Ballymore Inn, so for the time being it's business as usual
in this lovely bar and restaurant.

Business as usual is, of course, music to the ears of the
Ballymore's customers, who like things just exactly the
way they are: superb cooking, sweet surroundings, great
service, knockout value for money, great wines. Mrs
O'Sullivan has always been one of the great
contemporary cooks, her intellectual understanding of
Irish food put to brilliant use in the most delicious dishes:
Slaney lamb with courgette fritters; wild mushroom
risotto with char-grilled vegetables; steakburger with
crispy leeks and organic leaves; meringue with warm
berries and mascarpone cream. Best of all, Mrs O'Sullivan
lavishes the same thought and care on a sandwich or a
pizza as on the most elaborate main course, so
everything you eat is blessed with the utmost goodness.

● **OPEN:** 12.30pm-9pm Mon-Sun. 12.30pm-3pm
express lunch.
● **PRICE:** Lunch €25 Dinner €40, Express lunch
€12.50 for 2 courses
● **CREDIT CARDS:** All major cards accepted.

● **NOTES:**
♿ access.

● **DIRECTIONS:**
In the centre of Ballymore Eustace, on the right-hand
side of the road when coming from Blessington.

HUDSON'S

Richard and Kyra Hudson
Station Road, Thomastown
County Kilkenny
℡ **056-779 3900**
🖷 **056-779 3901**
✆ **hudsonsrestaurant@eircom.net**

Cleverly balancing conservative
cooking with hip style and service,
Hudson's is a pro team. Expect lots of
visiting golfers in Ryder Cup year.

Richard and Kyra Hudson's hip Thomastown address isn't
to everyone's taste – some of our editors reckon it is
fantastic, whilst others find it a little too self-conscious
for its own good, though that may be explained by the
presence of prosperous golfers moonlighting from Mount
Juliet, or celebs such as Ronan Keating – but the rock-
solid style of food and its calm simplicity, along with
elegant and luxurious dining rooms, explain why this
restaurant has been such a success from day one.
The menu is rather masculine in orientation – they cook
huge striploin steaks on the grill, along with meaty fish
such as halibut, which is served simply with lemon and
herb butter, and there is rump of lamb and bangers and
mash – but the conservatism of the style doesn't dampen
their flair, and dishes are pretty and composed. Hudson's
succeeds because, like Chez Hans in Cashel, for instance,
it is a restaurant that serves what its customers want to
eat, and it delivers with consistent flair and vital energy.

● **OPEN:** 6pm-10pm Tue-Sat; noon-8pm Sun (all day
lunch till 6pm, dinner 6pm-8pm)
● **PRICE:** Dinner €35
● **CREDIT CARDS:** All major cards accepted.

● **NOTES:**
♿ access.
Early Bird dinner, served until 7pm, €24.

● **DIRECTIONS:**
Hudson's is 170 metres up from SuperValu, on the road
travelling towards Mount Juliet.

ZUNI

**Paul & Paula Byrne, Sandra &
Alan McDonald
26 Patrick St, Kilkenny**
✆ **056-772 3999**
🖷 **056-775 6400**
🖰 **www.zuni.ie**

A smart new sandwich bar in the city shows the smart Zuni empire rolling out to conquer the globe.

The dynamic quartet operating Zuni have now opened Zuni Espress, a little further down the town on Rose Inn Street, so anyone who wants a blast of those zappy Zuni flavours but is pressed for time can now grab an excellent sandwich and a hot drink to go. The sandwiches show the same creative fervour that has made Zuni the Kilkenny hot spot, with fulsome assemblages such as the Irish – a belly-busting conglomeration of sausage, bacon, Clonakilty pudding and fried egg on a white bap (which deserves the cynic's title for the Irish breakfast – The Full catastrophe) – to elegant Japanese-style sandwiches with salmon and wasabi mayo. But, back up the street, Zuni continues to be the star attraction, a seductive and delightful modern Irish restaurant with rooms, and, under chef Maria Raftery, some marvellous, unpretentious cooking: beer-battered prawns with guacamole; duck confit with celeriac polenta; bacon loin with colcannon; lime and lemongrass torte. Classy food, classy operation.

● **OPEN:** 12.30pm-2.30pm, 6.30pm-9.30pm Mon-Sat; 1pm-2.45pm, 6pm-8.30pm Sun
● **PRICE:** Dinner €40-€45
● **CREDIT CARDS:** All major cards accepted.

● **NOTES:**
♿ access.
Early Bird dinner, Sun-Fri, €18.95-€25

● **DIRECTIONS:**
110 metres up Patrick Street from the main traffic junction at the road up to the Castle.

THE OARSMAN

Ronan & Conor Maher
Bridge Street
Carrick-on-Shannon
County Leitrim
© **071-962 1733**
🖰 **www.theoarsman.com**

The Maher brothers and
their kitchen crew are
delivering some of the most
exciting eating you can find.

In the last edition of this book, we wrote that "Chefs Sean
Hanna and Sheila Sharpe are producing some of the finest
cooking in the Midlands".

Well, scrap that, because Mr Hanna and Ms Sharpe are
now producing some of the best food in the country, as
Ronan and Conor Maher's dynamic restaurant and bar
powers ahead. The highest compliment we can pay Mr
Hanna's savoury cooking is to say that it puts us in mind
of contemporary Spanish cooking: it is vibrant with
colour and texture, it gives you energy as you work
through a dish such as chicken with mushroom duxelles
and Cooleeney camembert and polenta croquette, or
hake en papillote with cauliflower purée – and it provides
both comfort and culinary excitement. The sweet
cooking, such as a knockout apple and cinnamon crumble
with rhubarb and rosemary sorbet, is just as exiting, and
that is exactly what this kitchen is delivering: exciting
food, exciting eating, as The Oarsman coasts to greatness.

● **OPEN:** Lunch noon-3.30pm Mon-Wed; noon-2.30pm
Thurs-Sat; Dinner served 6.45pm-9.45pm Thurs-Sat.
● **PRICE:** Lunch €17, Dinner €40-€50.
● **CREDIT CARDS:** Mastercard/Visa

● **NOTES:**
No children in the bar after 9pm.

● **DIRECTIONS:**
The Oarsman is in the centre of Carrick-on-Shannon on
Bridge Street, 100 metres from the bridge over the
River Shannon.

COPPER & SPICE

**Seema & Bryan Conroy
2 Cornmarket Row
Limerick, County Limerick
© 061-313620
🖷 061-313922
www.copperandspice.com**

Seema and Bryan Conroy's Copper & Spice keeps on moving, constantly adapting new ideas and improving existing menus in a progressive way.

Bryan and Seema Conroy's Copper & Spice has trailblazed as an advocate of two types of ethnic cooking – Indian and Thai – over the last few years, with amazing success both commercially and culinarily. But Mrs Conroy isn't finished yet, for having spent several years living in Japan, she is keen to introduce some further Asian elements – ramen, teriyaki, yakitori, bulgogi and laksalemak.

This questing and adventurous spirit has been what has set C&S apart from other ethnic restaurants, who tend to hit a groove, and then stay there. Right from when they opened in Limerick, C&S has kept moving, altering menus to bring on new ideas, introducing special menus alongside the main menus in order that the kitchen can keep innovating. This continual progression should be a lesson to other ethnic restaurants. Visitors to the second C&S, at Annacotty, should note that it has moved to a waterside location above the Mill Bar.

- **OPEN:** 5pm-10.30pm Mon-Sun
- **PRICE:** Dinner €30
- **CREDIT CARDS:** All major cards accepted

- **NOTES:**
♿ access
Early Bird dinner, 5pm-7pm, €22.50

- **DIRECTIONS:**
Copper & Spice is overlooking the traditional Milk Market in the centre of Limerick city. Cornmarket Row runs across Mungret Street.

THE WILD GEESE

David Foley & Julie Randles
Rose Cottage, Main Street
Adare, County Limerick
☎ **061-396451**
🖷 **061-396451**
🖱 **www.thewild-geese.com**

The Wild Geese is stupendously pretty, but it is superb food and service that makes the WG so hot.

The prettiest restaurant in the prettiest house in the prettiest village in Ireland, that's The Wild Geese. Fortunately, there is more to the WG than just the pretty stuff. David Foley and Julie Randles are two of the leading exponents of the art of running a restaurant that you can find anywhere; his skills as a cook perfectly complemented by her skills as one of the supreme front-of-house operators. In fact, these guys don't even need all that pretty stuff: put them in a Nissen hut and food lovers would still be dazzled by their abilities, especially dishes such as monkfish with crabmeat and creamed spinach, or canon of lamb with black pudding mousse, or quail with chicory and orange, or dark chocolate tart.

What we like about the WG is how everything chimes, everything is of a piece. The food is just the right food for these intimate rooms, the service is just the right way of looking after you. And, after five years here in Adare, everything in the WG just gets better and better.

● **OPEN:** 6.30pm-10pm Tue-Sun (closed Sun off season)
● **PRICE:** Dinner €36
● **CREDIT CARDS:** Visa, Mastercard, Amex, Diners, Laser

● **NOTES:**
♿ access, but not to toilets.

● **DIRECTIONS:**
On the Main Street of Adare village, near the gates of Adare Manor and just opposite the Dunraven Arms Hotel. Look for the thatched roof.

CROCKET'S ON THE QUAY

Seamus Commons
Ballina
County Mayo
✆ **096-75930**
🖷 **096-70069**
🖱 **www.crocketsonthequay.ie**

Crocket's is the most rockin' restaurant and bar in the north west, packing in the punters for ace food.

Crocket's ought not to work, for anyone who wants to serve a complex menu in both restaurant and bar to one hundred and fifty punters on a weekend night ought to be doomed to failure. Yet Seamus Commons and his team pull it off, and do so with gas in the tank. Food and service in Crocket's get the job done with steely energy and efficiency, which mean it's not a problem not getting a table in the little restaurant, with its cool jazz photos, for the big, blousy bar has exactly the same level of cooking, and a livelier atmosphere.

So, we started with the ham hock and chicken confit terrine, served with toast and caramelised onions, and it was just right. Then we had wild sea trout – a fish as rare as hen's teeth – served with herb gnocchi, asparagus, peas and tomato concassé, and the dish was a harmonious success. So then we had a crème brûlée with rhubarb compote, and it was great. The place was leppin', and everyone seemed more than happy to be in Crocket's.

- **OPEN:** 6pm-9.30pm Mon-Sun
- **PRICE:** Dinner €25
- **CREDIT CARDS:** Visa, Mastercard, Amex, Diners

- **NOTES:**
♿ access. Bar food served 12.30pm-9pm. Bar lunch €20

- **DIRECTIONS:**
Take the Sligo road out of town, cross over the Bunree bridge and turn left at the traffic lights, then follow the river, and Crocket's is on the right-hand side.

10 RESTAURANTS
WITH GREAT MUSIC

1

CAFÉ PARADISO
CORK, Co CORK

2

CAYENNE
BELFAST, Co ANTRIM

3

COAST
TRAMORE, Co WATERFORD

4

ELY
DUBLIN, Co DUBLIN

5

FRANK'S BAR & RESTAURANT
DUBLIN, Co DUBLIN

6

GOOD THINGS CAFÉ
DURRUS, Co CORK

7

THE IVORY TOWER
CORK, Co CORK

8

JACQUES
CORK, Co CORK

9

THE LEFT BANK BISTRO
ATHLONE, Co WESTMEATH

10

THE MERMAID CAFÉ
DUBLIN, Co DUBLIN

THE RESTAURANT AT NUREMORE

Julie Gilhooly
Nuremore Hotel
Carrickmacross, Co Monaghan
© **042-966 1438,** ☎ **042-966 1853**
🖰 **www.nuremore-hotel.ie.**

Utter self-confidence allows Raymond McArdle to make complete sense of rich, grandstanding cooking.

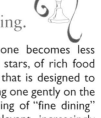

Is it simply a sign of ageing, that one becomes less interested in the world of chefs and stars, of rich food seen as a grand culinary panjandrum that is designed to show off cheffy technique whilst patting one gently on the bourgeois back? The old Escoffier thing of "fine dining" seems to us to be increasingly irrelevant, increasingly unattractive. We don't, to be perfectly honest, know what "fine dining" is, other than having a suspicion that it simply means being pretentious.

But, in the right hands, there are exceptions to this rule, and if you want grandstanding cooking, then Raymond McArdle is your man. Mr McArdle cooks for the stars, his work a rush of richness – turbot with scallops and velouté of lobster; foie gras with Sauternes jelly; Lincolnshire duck with foie gras; Angus beef with osso bucco choux farci; coulant of Valrhona with white chocolate fudge ice cream. He makes it work, because he isn't the tiniest bit self-conscious: he utterly believes in it.

● **OPEN:** 12.30pm-2.30pm, 6.30pm-9.30pm Mon-Sun (no lunch on Sat)
● **PRICE:** Lunch €25, Dinner €48-€80
● **CREDIT CARDS:** Visa, Mastercard, Amex, Diners

● **NOTES:**
♿ acces. - ramp from car park, no steps to restaurant.

● **DIRECTIONS:**
1.5km south of Carrickmacross on the principal N2, Dublin-Derry route, signposted at the entrance.

BROCKA ON THE WATER

Anthony & Anne Gernon
Kilgarvan Quay
Ballinderry
County Tipperary
℗ **067-22038**
🗏 **067-22955**

Brocka is the ultimate
luxury brand restaurant,
every detail handtooled and
utterly uncompromised.

Brocka has the magic. Whilst we describe this most
singular restaurant as a "luxury brand", in order to give
some idea of its sleek singularity, it would be just as easy
to say that in fact Brocka is the antithesis of the luxury
brand, simply because as a restaurant it is so personal.
No one else could do what Anne, Anthony and Nancy do
here, and no one else could do it half so well. If Brocka is
a luxury brand, it is a brand of one, a truly unique artefact,
a sport of nature that both defines the best of Irish food
and hospitality, and yet exists on its own in terms of Irish
food and hospitality.
Everything, from the room to the drinks to the place
settings to the serene and sublime cooking from Nancy,
is done with a precise aesthetic that melds artistry with
individuality. The spinach and garden vegetable soup is
painterly pretty and profound in flavour. The beef fillet
with fresh horseradish is elemental in its flavour and its
simplicity. Puddings are gorgeous, and Brocka is unique.

● **OPEN:** 7pm-10pm Mon-Sat. Reservations only.
● **PRICE:** Dinner €44
● **CREDIT CARDS:** No credit cards

● **NOTES:**
♿ access. Booking essential off season.
Creative cooking for children.

● **DIRECTIONS:**
On Kilgarvan Quay on the Lough Derg Drive, half way
between Nenagh and Portumna. From the N52, turn at
Borrisokane for Ballinderry.

CAFÉ HANS

Stefan & Hansi Matthiae
Moor Lane
Cashel
County Tipperary
℡ 0662-63660

Heard the one about the
parent trying to persuade
his children to eat chips?
No? Then read on...

In most restaurants, parents despair when their kids say, "I want the chips!". In Café Hans, it's the other way 'round. "We want the fresh beef bolognese with spaghetti, Parmesan and olive oil", say Connie and P.J.
"Well, okay, but you must, must, must try the chips, okay?" says Dad, as he orders bolognese x 2 and a plate of gnocchi with pancetta, ricotta and Parmesan cream for himself. The kids wolf down the delectable pasta, a cliché reinvented in Hans with amazing skill. The gnocchi is perfect, and very rich. "Try the chips, they're the best", says Dad. "But we're full," say Connie and P.J, "and we want dessert". "Well, just a few then, and we'll order the caramel ice cream, and I'll have the strawberries with passion fruit mousse and yogurt cream." The desserts are perfect, the room is gorgeous, the place is packed with families, and by 12.30pm people are already waiting 30 minutes for a table. That's Café Hans. They do everything differently, they do everything superbly, not just the chips.

- **OPEN:** noon-5.30pm Tue-Sat
- **PRICE:** Lunch main course €10-€13
- **CREDIT CARDS:** No credit cards

- **NOTES:**
♿ access.
No bookings taken.

- **DIRECTIONS:**
Two doors up from Chez Hans (opposite page), just beside the Rock of Cashel. Turn off the road at the junction at the Esso station.

CHEZ HANS

Jason Matthiae
Moor Lane
Cashel
County Tipperary
℡ **062-61177**
🖨 **062-61177**

Timeless cooking that mixes
the modern with the classic
makes Chez Hans one of the
truly great destinations.

Jason Matthiae's restaurant showcases not just the art of
contemporary Irish cooking, but also the art of
contemporary menu writing. Sit down in this glorious
converted church, open the menu, and you will suffer
agonies making a decision, because the menu is so
cleverly structured and expressed that you actually want
to eat everything – mushroom soup with tarragon cream;
char-grilled quail with Nicoise salad; risotto of wild
mushrooms with duckling; salmon with shrimp and spring
onion mash; scallops with pickled vegetable salad; lobster
grilled with lime, chilli and parsley butter; iced nougat
with almond praline; cinnamon roasted fruits with
mascarpone. Is there any solution to this dilemma? Well,
you can have tasting plates of starters and desserts, which
helps a little bit, but not much
 And if they can talk it, this kitchen sure can walk it, which
means we have never had a disappointing dish in Chez
Hans, far less a disappointing meal. A superb address.

● **OPEN:** 6pm-10pm Tue-Sat
● **PRICE:** Dinner €45.
● **CREDIT CARDS:** Visa, Mastercard

● **NOTES:**
♿ access.
Early Bird menu 6pm-7.15pm, €33

● **DIRECTIONS:**
Just beside the Rock of Cashel. The restaurant is clearly
signposted from the main N8, Dublin-Cork road; turn
off down the hill at the junction at the Esso station.

CLIFFORD'S

Michael & Deirdre Clifford
29 Thomas Street, Clonmel
County Tipperary
© **052-70677**
🖷 **052-70676**
🖑 **cliffordsrestaurant@eircom.net**

Cooking that is classic and elegant and timeless is Michael Clifford's signature style, producing food you can simply never tire of.

"Imagination, love, fresh ingredients locally sourced." That's what it says on the top of the menus in Michael Clifford's restaurant, and that is what you get every time this great exemplar and veteran of the Irish kitchen fires up the stoves. What you also get with Mr Clifford's cooking is a continuing sense of enquiry, for this cook has never lost his hunger for new ideas and directions in the kitchen, which means that his menus are composed equally of his classic dishes – gâteau of Clonakilty black pudding; cassoulet of lamb's liver and kidney; quenelle of chicken with Milleens; his signature Irish stew; chicken with apples and almonds – abetted with new ideas, like spiced chicken kebabs with peppers and courgettes, or plaice with coconut, ginger and chilli, or Tipperary lamb with pear. Whatever he cooks, Mr Clifford makes both harmonious and subtle; timeless cooking that shows imagination, love, and respect for local foods. It's a lovely room; value for the early bird and Sunday lunch is ace.

- **OPEN:** 12.30pm-2.30pm Tue-Fri; 12.30pm-4pm Sun; 6.30pm-10pm Tue-Sun
- **PRICE:** Lunch €8-€14, Dinner €45-€50
- **CREDIT CARDS:** Visa, Mastercard

- **NOTES:**
♿ access.
Sunday lunch recommended for families.
Early Bird dinner menu, 5pm-8pm, €26.50.

- **DIRECTIONS:**
Near the railway station, near the centre of Clonmel.

GANNON'S ABOVE THE BELL

Dermot Gannon
2 Pearse Street
Cahir
County Tipperary
✆ **052-45911**

Dermot Gannon's restaurant is one of the dynamos of Tipp's dynamic restaurant culture, with some of the most creative food in the Midlands.

Tipperary is becoming one of the gastronomic centres of cooking in Ireland – just look at the stellar standards of the entries in this book, their individuality and their hungry excellence. It's a competitive food culture that suits the talents of Dermot Gannon perfectly, for this guy can hold his head amongst any collection of super chefs, and in the pretty Gannon's he proves his mettle at every service, Of course, he is blessed with truly great suppliers, who help him to create one of the country's finest Road Map menus – and whose names he lists on the menu. And Mr Gannon seizes on these foods to produce stonking cooking: Ballybrado organic pork salad with Crozier Blue cheese; Bluebell Falls goat's cheese with roasted vegetables; crispy duck breast with Traas plum jelly; Tipperary lamb Kashmiri style; Whelan's 21-day old sirloin with whiskey pepper cream. The early bird menus are amongst the best value you can find, perfect if you are navigating the N7/N8.

● **OPEN:** 5.30pm-9pm Tue-Sun, (until 9.30pm Fri-Sat). Closed Mon & Tues off season.
● **PRICE:** Dinner €40
● **CREDIT CARDS:** Visa, Mastercard

● **NOTES:**
Gannon's bar food served at The Bell. ♿ access to bar, not restaurant. Early Bird dinner 5.30pm-6.30pm Mon-Sat; 5pm-8pm Sun, €26.

● **DIRECTIONS:**
Near to the town's main square, upstairs over the pub.

LILY MAI'S

Frances Fogarty, Feargal O Cinneide
Thomastown
Golden, Cashel
County Tipperary
© 062-72847
🖱 www.lilymais.com

Lily Mai's adventurous and imaginative country cooking is quickly making waves in Tipperary.

The Lily Mai's trio of owners Frances Fogarty and Fergal Ó Cinnéide and chef Declan Hayes are making waves in Golden, a tiny hamlet where their converted stone cottage is the new destination for Tipp's food lovers. The rooms are cleverly designed and atmospheric, the Fixed Mark Up strategy on wines will persuade you to order a super bottle, and even before Mr Hayes' precise food begins to arrive you sense this trio have things right.

The food enjoys strong flavours, and a genuine sense of enquiry: one evening, tiger prawns and scallops come as a main course with a chervil guacamole and a brandy and prawn sauce. Another night, they will be a starter, cooked on a brochette with a sweet chilli sauce. Simple dishes such as Tipperary lamb with a honey and herb crust, or house-smoked mackerel with potato salad and salsa verde are perfect, and desserts are strong: Traas' strawberries with mascarpone; chocolate and pear tart. The veg cookery needs work, but Lily Mai's is humming.

- ● **OPEN:** 6.30pm-10pm Wed-Sat
- ● **PRICE:** Dinner €48
- ● **CREDIT CARDS:** Visa, Mastercard, Diners

● **NOTES:**
♿ access. Reservation highly recommended. The restaurant has a policy of not turning tables. Your table is yours for the night.

● **DIRECTIONS:**
In Thomastown village, which is on the main Cashel to Tipperary road.

BODEGA!

Cormac & Donagh Cronin
54 John Street
Waterford
County Waterford
© **051-844177**
🖰 **www.bodegawaterford.com**

Cormac and Donagh Cronin's Bodega
has been undergoing design and
staffing changes, but the sheer energy
and joie de vivre of this bar remains.

The Cronin brothers' Bodega has had a few kitchen
changes, along with some structural alterations, during
the year, pressures that introduced some inconsistencies
which have now been put to rest as they focus on
working with the redesigned kitchen and just getting the
food out. What hasn't changed is the magnificently
raucous atmosphere that this mighty pub can
manufacture pretty much any night of the week – Bodega
is one of those places that even if the food did slip an iota,
you could easily forgive it, simply because you were so
swept up in the wild buzz of wild Waterford city.
But when the food hits the spot, the combination of food,
value and craic is pretty irresistible; a sublime alchemy of
ingredients no other place can concoct. It's food that puts
flavour first – Landoise salad with foie gras on bruschetta;
Toulouse sausage with mash is straight-ahead, no-
nonsense bistro grub, whilst veal liver can be as ethereal
as the most delicate dim sum. Excellent value, super fun.

● **OPEN:** noon-2.30pm Mon-Fri; 5.30pm-10pm Mon-
Wed; 5.30pm-10.30pm Thu-Sat
● **PRICE:** Lunch €6.50-€15, Dinner €34
● **CREDIT CARDS:** Visa, Mastercard, Laser

● **NOTES:**
♿ access.
Early Bird 5.30pm-7pm Mon-Fri, €23.

● **DIRECTIONS:**
Just down from the apple market right in the centre of
Waterford city, adjacent to the Cork Rd multi-storey.

COAST

Turlough McNamara & Jenny McNally
Upper Branch Road
Tramore, County Waterford
℡ **051-393646**
🖶 **051-393647**
🖰 **www.coast.ie**

Eugene Long's classic and
stylish cooking has kept
Coast rockin' all year, in
one of the best destinations.

Turlough McNamara and Jenny McNally, having established Coast as one of the key south-east destinations, have now also opened the stylish 33 in Waterford city, along with Shoebaloo, which has to be the funkiest shoe shop in the country.

That's the measure of these guys. They are pioneers, people who take an idea – in the case of Coast, to have a rockin' restaurant with superb rooms upstairs – they make it work, and having seen that it runs smooth as clockwork, they seize the next idea. Most people can't run one restaurant properly, but McNamara and McNally are expert at getting dedicated people to work with them, and they know how to unlock potential. The desserts in Coast, for instance, are demon concoctions, but they are made by the guy who started as a plongeur. Meantime, Eugene Long keeps this kitchen rockin' along, and one dinner with a friend and one dinner with the family in Coast showed a kitchen on searing, tip-top form.

- **OPEN:** 6.30pm-10pm Tue-Sat; 1pm-3pm Sun
- **PRICE:** Dinner €35-€40
- **CREDIT CARDS:** Visa, Mastercard, Amex, Laser

- **NOTES:**
♿ access. Rooms available in Townhouse, €50-€80 per person sharing. Early Bird dinner €26.50 served 6pm-7.30pm Tue-Fri.

- **DIRECTIONS:**
Just up from the beach front road in Tramore, the entrance is on Upper Branch Road.

RICHMOND HOUSE

Paul & Claire Deevy
Cappoquin
County Waterford
✆ **058-54278**
🖷 **058-54988**
🖱 **www.richmondhouse.net**

Paul and Claire Deevy's Richmond House is the most quintessentially Irish of modern restaurants.

Richmond House is one of the great addresses in Ireland because it is one of the great Irish addresses. The welcome, the greeting, the demureness, the understated style, the warmly burning fire – even in August – is all a reminder of how superbly Irish people – and most especially Paul and Claire Deevy – both understand and understand how to deliver hospitality. Staying and eating in Richmond gives you a glimpse into the Irish soul.

Fortunately, with Mr Deevy in the kitchen it also shows you exactly what is going on with the Irish tummy. And very fine it is too; a careful, gentle exercise in cooking that is dedicated to flavour, to goodness, to pleasure. A tempura of helvick prawns comes with just-right pickled cucumber, whilst wild Blackwater salmon has superb scallops and fresh asparagus. Children are specially catered for, there is a superb menu for vegetarians, the service under Claire Deevy is as good as it gets, and Richmond all adds up to a special magic, an Irish magic.

- **OPEN:** 7pm-9pm Mon-Sun (closed Sun off season)
- **PRICE:** Dinner €48
- **CREDIT CARDS:** Visa, Mastercard, Amex, Diners

- **NOTES:**
Recommended for vegetarians. ♿ access with assistance. Early Bird 6.30pm-7.30pm €30.

- **DIRECTIONS:**
Just outside the town of Cappoquin, heading in the direction of Waterford city, and clearly signposted from the main road.

THE TANNERY RESTAURANT

Paul and Máire Flynn,
10 Quay Street, Dungarvan
County Waterford
✆ **058-45420**
🖷 **058-45814**
🖑 **www.tannery.ie**

Paul Flynn's food is as smart and original as contemporary Irish cooking gets: don't miss the thrill.

"Richly satisfying for the body and the brain", was what we scribbled on the back of the menu after lunch in The Tannery, along with a whole heap of outrageous praise which failed to do justice to the superb meal we had enjoyed with the family in a packed, pumping restaurant. And it's that "brain" bit that is important, for we also noted that Paul Flynn's cooking "eschews fashion, but always spins something new out of the ingredients". And that is the secret of The Tannery: other chefs rarely create and are by-and-large content to copy the same ideas with their dishes. But Paul Flynn is forever making his own, original, unique signatures with everything: cotechino sausage with roast chicken; candied almonds with smoked chicken; Asian-style vegetables with belly of pork, Crozier Blue cheese with a warm ham hock salad, or confecting crab meat into a crème brûlée. This cooking is so exciting that if you go for lunch you want to come back for dinner. Do note there are now splendid rooms for overnighting.

● **OPEN:** 12.30pm-2.15pm Tue-Fri & Sun; 6.30pm-9.30pm Tue-Sat; (6pm-9pm Sun Jul-Aug & bank holidays)
● **PRICE:** Lunch €26, Dinner €45-€50
● **CREDIT CARDS:** Visa, Mastercard, Amex, Diners

● **NOTES:**
♿ access. Early Bird dinner, 6.30pm-7.30pm Tue-Fri, €27. Bridgestone 100 Best Places to Stay recommends The Tannery guesthouse nearby.

● **DIRECTIONS:**
Situated beside the Old Market House building.

33 THE MALL

**Turlough McNamara,
Tom & Brian Drohan
33 The Mall
Waterford**
✆ **051-859823**
🖱 **www.33.ie**

north

east

west

south

Another wowee! success
address from Turlough
McNamara. We say: make
this guy Taoiseach, today.

33 The Mall is the most gorgeous building, just around the
corner from Waterford's esplanade, and it's the latest
scheme to be blessed by the meticulous attentions of
Turlough McNamara, best known for his Tramore
restaurant and rooms, Coast.

As with Coast, 33 is ultra cool, a slice of the zeitgeist that
once again raises the style bar higher than before. "It's like
Marie Antoinette's drawing room" said one local food
lover. "You have to stick your head out the door to
remind yourself you are still in Waterford." But 33 isn't
just modish, post-Wallpaper* style. The simple menu has
delivered from day one, a style of food you might eat in
some London hotspot such as the Wolseley: chicken and
leek pie; lobster mayonnaise; dressed crab; eggs benedict;
Angus hamburger: prawn scampi with fries and tartare.
This textbook brasserie food gets textbook delivery, with
as much attention paid to proper cocktails and drinks as
the food receives. Let them eat brioche, is what we say.

● **OPEN:** 5.30pm-late Mon-Sat; 11am-7pm Sun
● **PRICE:** Mains €12-€25, Sun brunch mains
€12-€18
● **CREDIT CARDS:** Visa, Mastercard, Laser

● **NOTES:**
♿ access. Reservation unnecessary.
Private room 15-20 people.

● **DIRECTIONS:**
33 is a landmark building in the centre of Waterford,
just across from the Theatre Royal.

WATERFORD CASTLE

Michael Quinn
Waterford Castle, The Island
Ballinakill, County Waterford
✆ **051-878203**
🖨 **051-871634**
🖱 **www.waterfordcastle.com**

Ignore the fussy, formal, flootery stuff about Waterford Castle: what you are here for is Michael Quinn's brilliant, red-hot contemporary cooking.

Overlooking the naff things about Waterford Castle – the stuffy formality, the jacket-and-tie requirement, the over-formal service – is simple, simply because Michael Quinn is one of the best chefs in Ireland.

This guy wrings flavours out of food that just knock you for six – his trio of crab with a crab brûlée, a crab spring roll and a tian with pickled cucumber; a megatastic rump of lamb with a startling cumin jus; lobster a l'Americaine with pea purée; fantastic banana, chocolate and hazelnut parfait – are just some of the latest dishes to which Mr Quinn brings a triumphant creativity that balances great technique with a wild and playful streak. This cooking is as far from hotel dining room food as you can get, and is amongst the most enjoyable cooking you can find. We wish things were less regimented in the 'Castle – surely the rich Americans get enough of that blather at home without wanting it on their holidays – but if Michael Quinn were cooking in a Nissen hut, that would be fine.

● **OPEN:** 7pm-8.30pm Mon-Sun (open till 9pm Fri & Sat)
● **PRICE:** Dinner €58 + 10% service charge
● **CREDIT CARDS:** Visa, Mastercard, Amex, Diners

● **NOTES:**
♿ access.

● **DIRECTIONS:**
5 km out of Waterford on the Dunmore East Road. They operate their own ferry to the island.

THE LEFT BANK BISTRO

Annie McNamara & Mary McCullagh
Fry Place, Athlone
County Westmeath
✆ **090-649 4446**
🖷 **090-649 4509**
🖱 **www.leftbankbistro.com**

Michael Durr's voluptuous
modern cooking in the
lovely Left Bank Bistro is
irresistibly delicious.

"The best meal I enjoyed all year," was how Colm
Conyngham, marketing manager of Bridgestone Ireland,
and a chap with whom we have worked on the
Bridgestone Guides since 1991, described his last trip to
Annie and Mary's Left Bank Bistro, a sleek room in the
heart of old Athlone.
No surprise there. This dynamic, creative and energised
room is the star of the Midlands, and with Michael Durr
in the kitchen firing on all cylinders, the food is simply an
ode to deliciousness – Blackwater valley gravadlax with
mustard and dill and caper berries; chorizo and
mushroom bruschetta with Parmesan; Asian-marinated
duck with apple and mint salsa; Hereford sirloin with
melting garlic and parsley butter. Mr Durr melds the
Asian-Australian influences of Annie and Mary with his
own ruddy signature, and the result is powerfully
flavoured food that knocks you for six. The room is one
of the most beautiful, and the atmosphere is life-affirming.

● **OPEN:** 10.30am-9.30pm (lunch served noon-5pm,
dinner served 5.30pm-close Tue-Sat)
● **PRICE:** Main course lunch €11.50, Dinner €40
● **CREDIT CARDS:** Visa, Mastercard, Amex

● **NOTES:**
♿ access. Early Bird menu 5.30pm-7.30pm Tue-Fri, €25

● **DIRECTIONS:**
Behind the castle in the old town of Athlone, The Left
Bank is on the west side of the Shannon, on the corner
of the steep Fry Place.

FORDE'S

Liam Forde
The Crescent
Wexford
County Wexford
℅ 053-23832
📠 053-23832

Maximum flavours, in what is otherwise an age of minimalist cooking, are what sets Liam Forde's popular restaurant apart from others.

The cooking in Liam Forde's eponymous restaurant is as busy and as convoluted as the decor. But whilst we aren't mad on the decor – save for greatly admiring the fastidious housekeeping – we are as keen on Mr Forde's cooking as the citizens of Wexford town.

His food is cheffy, and intense, but somehow it never gets too complicated for its own good. Mr Forde wants to deliver value and generosity, so he will garnish lemon sole with crab claws, he will put mussels with monkfish and some asparagus, he will place a fritter of brie on the plate with fillet steak, whilst chicken can have brie, bacon and roast garlic. This all adds up to punchy, special-occasion cooking, and whilst it is not fashionable in its complexity, Mr Forde makes it work. You might describe his cooking as culinary maximalism in an age of culinary minimalism, a relic, perhaps, of cordon bleu cookery. What you call it doesn't matter a toss: it works, it's tasty, and the Forde's crew are right up for it, delivering good times every night.

- **OPEN:** 6pm-10pm Mon-Sun; noon-10pm Sun
- **PRICE:** Sun lunch €24, Dinner €35-€40
- **CREDIT CARDS:** All major cards accepted

- **NOTES:**
♿ access.
Early Bird dinner, 6pm-7pm, €23.20.

- **DIRECTIONS:**
In the centre of Wexford town, on the waterfront.
Forde's is on the Crescent Quay front, just opposite the John Barry memorial statue.

LA MARINE

**Eugene Callaghan
Kelly's Resort Hotel
Rosslare, County Wexford**
℡ **053-32114**
🖷 **053-32222**
⌂ **www.kellys.ie**

Quietly and stealthily, Eugene Callaghan has rewritten the bistro rules all on his own in La Marine.

Take all the great classic bistro and brasserie dishes – ham hock terrine; potato salad with cured herring; cod with brandade in piquillo; coq au vin with button mushrooms; lamb shank with almonds; sirloin with gratin dauphinois; grilled mussels with garlic and parsley butter; duck confit; meringue with hot chocolate sauce; cappuccino crème brûlée – and Eugene Callaghan cooks them all better than anyone else working in Ireland.

His cooking is both respectfully within the tradition, and also outside the tradition, because he has made these culinary clichés into works of art and, thereby, he has made them his very own. No one else's food is quite so pure, so seemingly simple. He is quite simply an awe-inspiring chef, a cook who reaches the parts of culinary concoctions that others don't even realise are there.

He has a great room in which to work, a great team all around him, and a great wine list to complement his food. It adds up to a pitch-perfect, top-of-his-game restaurant.

● **OPEN:** 12.30pm-2.15pm, 6.30pm-9.30pm Mon-Sun. Closed Dec-end Feb
● **PRICE:** Lunch/snack menu €7-€15, Dinner €34
● **CREDIT CARDS:** Visa, Mastercard, Amex

● **NOTES:**
♿ access with advance notice.

● **DIRECTIONS:**
Kelly's Hotel is well signposted from in the area. La Marine has a separate entrance on the left side of the hotel as you stand facing the front.

AVOCA

The Pratt family
● **Kilmacanogue, County Wicklow**
Tel: (01) 286 7466 ● **Suffolk St,**
Dublin 2 Tel: (01) 672 6019
● **Powerscourt House, Enniskerry,**
Co Wicklow Tel: (01) 204 6070

The Avoca cafés are
amongst the very nicest
places to eat on your own:
time dedicated to you.

There can be a lot of eating on your own involved in
writing about a restaurant culture, and most of it isn't
that much fun. Yes the food can be good, the food can be
great, but eating in a restaurant is a sociable activity, and
behaving in a monastic fashion isn't really what
restaurants are all about.

And yet, one of the things we like about Avoca is the fact
that it is the most splendid series of restaurants in which
to eat on your own. In Wicklow recently, we had the Thai
chicken with basmati rice, some sweet and lovely carrot
salad, some beetroot, and some pea, feta and spinach. It
was a smashing lunch, en route to a meeting. Another
time, we stopped off at Bunratty en route to West Cork
on a Sunday late morning, and had some lovely potato
and parsley soup, good crumbly brown bread, and a cup
of coffee, and we were recharged for the road. Avoca
makes those experiences special, because no detail
eludes them, nothing is too small for their careful eye.

● **OPEN:** 9.30am-5pm Mon-Sun
● **PRICE:** Lunch €10-€18
● **CREDIT CARDS:** All major cards accepted

● **NOTES:**
Good ♿ access in Kilmacanogue.

● **DIRECTIONS:**
Kilmacanogue is on the N11. For Powerscourt follow
signs to the gardens. Suffolk Street is in the centre of
Dublin, at the lower end of Grafton Street.

GRANGECON CAFÉ

Richard & Jenny Street
Tullow Road
Blessington
County Wicklow
☎ **045-857892**
✆ **grangeconcafe@eircom.net**

Richard and Jenny and their
crew take everything back to
basic goodness in the sublime
and brilliant Grangecon Café.

Why is Grangecon so good? Well, to understand this crew, and how they work, let's look at their sausage roll, a food that normally speaks of the worst excesses of mechanised farming and industrialised food production.
In Grangecon, they source organic pork from Jens Krumpe, an exemplary organic farmer. They make their own puff pastry (!), the onion used with the pork is organic, and there is just a little bit of salt and pepper and some herbs. "I will put that into competition with anything", says Richard Street, proudly. In our book, the Grangecon sausage roll doesn't need competition: it's the winner, by a mile. And, so is everything else here; the organic salads; the red pepper and goat's cheese tart; the organic scrambled eggs with Grangecon toast for breakfast, the tuna salad made with their own mayonnaise; the lemon tart, and the lovely wines they now source from Simon Tyrell. This is food taken to its elemental goodness, and Grangecon food makes us smile.

● **OPEN:** 9am-5.30pm Mon-Sat (4pm Mon).
Closed Sunday.
● **PRICE:** Lunch €10-15, Breakfast €7
● **CREDIT CARDS:** Visa, Mastercard, Laser

● **NOTES:**
♿ access. Child-friendly sandwiches.

● **DIRECTIONS:**
Blessington is on the N81 route south of Dublin to Enniscorthy. Heading south, turn left at the second set of traffic lights in the village: Grangecon is on the left.

THE STRAWBERRY TREE

Evan Doyle
Macreddin Village, Aughrim
County Wicklow
℡ **0402-36444**
🖷 **0402-36580**
🖰 **www.brooklodge.com**

Think of a single word to describe
The Strawberry Tree and its parent,
The Brook Lodge. Go on, then read
on and see what our one word is...

Think of one word that will explain the success of Evan
Doyle's revolutionary Brook Lodge Hotel, and its
iconoclastic Strawberry Tree restaurant. What will that
word be? It will be: Sensual.

In double-quick time, Mr Doyle and his team have
created, from a green-field site, an address that seems
age-old, but yet which seems utterly of the moment in
terms of its embrace of the modern zeitgeist of Ireland.
What is that zeitgeist? To enjoy space and food in a
meaningful, original way, to feel at one with where you
are, what you are doing, what you are eating.

In this regard, Frederic Souty's cooking in the restaurant
chimes perfectly with Mr Doyle's modus operandi. Wild
foods and organic foods are treated with respect and
consideration, and used in an holistic fashion. The flavours
and textures are unlike any other restaurant in Ireland,
yet they are totally at one with The Brook Lodge. That is
why the word is Sensual, because the sensuality is total.

● **OPEN:** 7pm-9.30pm Mon-Sat; 1pm-3.30pm Sun
● **PRICE:** Lunch €30, Dinner €55
● **CREDIT CARDS:** All major cards accepted

● **NOTES:**
♿ access. Macreddin Village encompasses the Brook
Lodge hotel, a market, shop, pub and Spa.

● **DIRECTIONS:**
From Aughrim follow the signpost to Macreddin Village
(3km). They will send detailed directions if requested:
good idea!

ALDEN'S

Jonathan Davis
229 Upper Newtownards Road
Belfast
County Antrim
℘ **028-9065 0032**
⌐ **www.aldensrestaurant.com**

Rigorous consistency and
punky creativity underlie
the glamorous experience
of eating at Alden's.

Alden's offers a sublime restaurant experience, thanks to
Cath Gradwell's inspired cooking and Jonathan Davis's
inspired management of this lovely room. It works as well
as it does because this pair have a natural generosity that
sets the tone of this stylish, confident space. The food is
generous in flavour, from classics like Dover sole with
shellfish sauce, to rabbit stuffed with cotechino sausage,
to squid with black beans, to summer pudding. And no
matter what she cooks, Ms Gradwell manages to make
something both utterly classical and yet individually
punky. Like the best female chefs, her cooking isn't
didactic: technique takes second place to a very personal
exploration of the culinary canon, but it is delivered with
a consistent excellence that is matched by few other
cooks. Mr Davis, meantime, is one of the great hosts,
leading his team by gracious example. Alden's never rests
on its laurels, and the fire in its belly is your guarantee of
a sublime, modern, signature dining experience.

● **OPEN:** noon-2.30pm Mon-Fri; 6pm-10pm Mon-Sat
(till 11pm Fri & Sat)
● **PRICE:** Lunch £5.95-£15, Dinner £30
● **CREDIT CARDS:** All major cards accepted.

● **NOTES:**
♿ access. Special Dinner menu, £17.95 for 2-courses
served Mon-Thu.

● **DIRECTIONS:**
On the Upper Newtownards Road, near the cross
roads with Sandown Road.

PAUL ARTHURS

Paul Arthurs
66 Main Street
Kircubbin
County Down
ⓒ **028-4273 8192**
🖰 **www.paul/arthurs.com**

Top-class ingredients meet with top-class cooking in Paul Arthurs' colourful upstairs bistro in Kircubbin, a showcase for contemporary cooking.

Foie gras, lobster, venison and partridge are seasonal staples at Paul Arthurs', but this doesn't mean you have to dress up. Anything goes at this bright, laid-back brasserie, run by a fiercely independent one-man band in the kitchen, along with a few bright young waitresses. Come here after a day on the lough, although people will travel miles just to eat Arthurs' chunky smoked haddock chowder, with its milky chive-flecked liquor, his cracked crab claws dripping with a hot butter of lemon, garlic and chilli, his billowy gnocchi with Gorgonzola cream. Then comes a whack of sirloin, all the better for Arthurs' butchery background, char-grilled and oozing with a spiced Café de Paris butter, pink honey-roast duck with shiitake, thick soy and sake, or some amazing catch of the day – turbot, Strangford prawns, Dover sole, all treated with the same flavour-focused flair. Desserts are dead simple and deadly. And you can crash for the night in Mr Arthur's smart new rooms upstairs. You may well need to.

- ● **OPEN:** 5pm-9pm Tue-Sat; noon-2.30pm Sun
- ● **PRICE:** Sun Lunch & Dinner £28
- ● **CREDIT CARDS:** Visa, Mastercard

● **NOTES:**
No wheelchair access, though there is a stair lift for disabled. Accommodation available, £70 double, £50 single. £10 supplement for children sharing.

● **DIRECTIONS:**
Right in the middle of main street in the village, on the left-hand side as you drive towards Portaferry.

CAYENNE

Paul & Jeanne Rankin
7 Ascot House, Shaftesbury Sq,
Belfast, County Antrim
© **028-9033 1532**
028-9026 1575
www.rankingroup.co.uk

In the funky Cayenne, Lemon Jelly is found on the soundtrack, and not on the dessert menu. Mind you, it might be nice to see lemon jelly on a menu.

Danny Millar's cooking in the groovy Cayenne is as post-modern as the design and style of this glamorous, artistically-conceived space, the sort of abstractly constructed and lit room where, whenever Lemon Jelly suddenly appear on the soundtrack, it doesn't come as any sort of surprise. The only surprise is that there isn't a lemon jelly pud on the dessert menu. Lamb chops are done Korean style, for example, and served with kim chee and roasted potatoes. Salt and chilli squid comes with Asian slaw and a pair of dipping sauces. Here and there dishes are delivered in classic format – basil and ricotta gnocchi is a textbook dish, for instance, served simply with roasted yellow tomatoes, but Cayenne's signature style, for the most part is iconoclastic, and we rather like the fact that they like to rip up the rule book and deconstruct their fave dishes. The restaurant itself has grown mightily in size over the years, which can put pressure on front-of-house staff at busy weekends.

● **OPEN:** noon-2.30pm Mon-Fri; 6pm-10.15pm Mon-Thur; 6pm-11.15pm Fri & Sat; 5pm-9pm Sun
● **PRICE:** Lunch £12-£17, Dinner from £15.50-£19.50
● **CREDIT CARDS:** Amex, Visa, Mastercard, Diners, Switch

● **NOTES:**
♿ access.

● **DIRECTIONS:**
At the top of Great Victoria Street in the city centre, Cayenne is easy to find in Shaftesbury Square.

DEANE'S BRASSERIE

**Michael Deane
38-40 Howard Street,
Belfast, County Antrim**
✆ **028-9056 0000**
🖱 **www.deanesbelfast.com**

Derek Creagh's arrival in
Deane's Brasserie has
brought vividly delicious
cooking back to the DB.

The formal, fine-dining experience of Restaurant Michael
Deane isn't really Bridgestone territory, but downstairs in
the Brasserie, you will find the sort of informal creativity
that rings our bell. Derek Creagh has worked with
Heston Blumenthal, but happily the talented, modest chef
is steering clear of molecular cooking, and is instead
drawing on the principles and skills learned from English
gastro-pubs and cheffy stars to produce some of the
most lip-licking menus Deane's Brasserie has served in
years. What's more, he's one of too few cooks innovating
with local ingredients. Cured fillet of mackerel comes
with escabeche and a tapenade crouton; chicken with
creamed Savoy, macaroni, lardons and tarragon jus; cider
braised belly of pork with langoustines, colcannon and
clonakilty blackpudding; smoked cod with champ, parsley
sauce and crispy pancetta. DB is great for light lunches,
when soups and tarts are knocked out with the same
panache, and this is delicious, handsome, well-priced food.

● **OPEN:** noon-3pm Mon-Sat; 5.30pm-10pm Mon-Thur;
5.30pm-11pm Fri & Sat
● **PRICE:** Lunch £25, Dinner £30-£35
● **CREDIT CARDS:** Visa, Mastercard, Amex, Switch

● **NOTES:**
♿ access.

● **DIRECTIONS:**
Howard Street is at the rere of the City Hall in the
centre of Belfast, as you walk down towards the Opera
House, DB is on the left hand side.

DIM SUM RESTAURANT

Oliver Tong
82 Botanic Avenue
Belfast
County Antrim
✆ **028-9043 9590**

Oliver Tong's restaurant now concentrates its focus on dim sum, with divine, ethereal culinary results.

Okay, so it's never going to be possible to get a table in Ferran Adria's El Bulli restaurant in Spain. So, what's the solution? The answer is to eat the fantastic dim sum in Oliver Tong's Dim Sum restaurant and, thereby, get yourself a blast of the ethereality, the textured surprise, the shock of the new, in which Adria specialises.

And when you do have the fantastic dim sum this kitchen delivers, from the lightest scallop dumplings to the ruddy, slightly chewy pork intestine to the fascinating and provocative satay tripe to the elegant, slithery beef rice rolls, you come to realise that what Adria is doing is nothing new, and that dim sum has always been about playing games with the textures and expectations of food. It's a pure thrill to eat here, and the secret to getting the best dim sum is to tell the charming waitresses that you want the dishes written in Chinese script at the foot of the menu, rather than the more conventional dishes concocted for conservative eaters. Ab Fab D S.

● **OPEN:** noon-10pm Mon-Thu, noon-midnight Fri & Sat; 11am-10pm Sun
● **PRICE:** dim sum prices range from £2.80-£3.20, local Chinese dishes start from £6.80, Cantonese specials are £8-£10.
● **CREDIT CARDS:** Visa, Mastercard

● **NOTES:**
No ♿ access.

● **DIRECTIONS:**
Botanic Avenue is in the University area of Belfast city.

10 RESTAURANTS
WITH GREAT STYLE

1

COAST
TRAMORE, Co WATERFORD

2

L'ECRIVAIN
DUBLIN, Co DUBLIN

3

FONTANA
HOLYWOOD, Co DOWN

4

GOOD THINGS CAFE
DURRUS, Co CORK

5

JAMES STREET SOUTH
BELFAST, Co ANTRIM

6

LA MARINE
ROSSLARE, Co WEXFORD

7

THE TANNERY
DUNGARVAN, CO WATERFORD

8

33 THE MALL
WATERFORD, CO WATERFORD

9

TOWN BAR & GRILL
DUBLIN, Co DUBLIN

10

ZUNI
KILKENNY, Co KILKENNY

THE DUKE RESTAURANT

Ciaran Gallagher
The Duke Bar
7 Duke Street
Warrenpoint, County Down
☎ **028-4175 2084**
🖰 **www.thedukerestaurant.com**

Ciaran Gallagher's The Duke
Restaurant is Warrenpoint's star of the
County Down, a rockin', creative
restaurant for sublime fish cookery.

Ciaran Gallagher loves seafood, and it shows. If he's not
out on a moonlit night collecting razor clams, he'll be up
the next day to see the fishermen on the pier.
As well as a discerning buyer, he's an enthusiastic chef,
seeking out new recipes, concentrating on good stocks
and sauces, navigating his own signature style as he steers
The Duke to ever-greater acclaim. For the "I-don't-eat-
fish" crowd there's a chicken Kiev and steak menu, with
sauces and stuffings cooked from scratch, but really it's a
sin to go there with the quality of seafood on offer.
Mussel and saffron broth, crab-filled courgette flowers,
and the Duke's legendary prawns with garlic, chilli, and
basil cream are for starters. Follow with a heaped seafood
grill of brill, hake, monkfish, prawns and crab, doused in a
buttery stock of lemon, shiitake mushrooms and garlic, or
hake with braised leeks, and a velouté thickened with
blended mussels. You will be stuffed to the gills but don't
on any account miss the fab, delicious desserts.

● **OPEN:** 6.30pm-10pm Tue-Sat; 5.30pm-9pm Sun
● **PRICE:** Dinner £22
● **CREDIT CARDS:** All major cards accepted

● **NOTES:**
♿ access to bar only. Bar lunch served noon-2pm Tue-
Sat, £4.50. Mid-week special dinner menu £13.50 for
3-courses.

● **DIRECTIONS:**
From Newry, 9.5km on the A2. Just off the square in the
centre of Warrenpoint, upstairs from the Duke bar.

FERNDALE

Peter Mills
Irvinestown Road, Enniskillen
County Fermanagh
© 028-6632 8374
🖰 www.ferndalecountry-
houseandrestaurant.com

Peter Mills has ambition and
ability, and has already made
significant advances in the
very promising Ferndale.

Peter Mills is ambitious and his ambition shows in both the changes he has made to Ferndale's decor – though there is still some way to go to get the entire aesthetic right, as he happily acknowledges – and in his cooking, which is volatile and imaginative. He will serve a course of curried monkfish with a shot glass of lager, for example, a nice, smart touch; he will freeze a kir royale as a sorbet course to give it extra oomph!, and elsewhere he relishes taking dishes apart in the modern style – salmon cured in Earl Grey tea; duck five ways; canon of lamb with confit shoulder and sweetbread beignet; a bouillabaisse risotto style with sea bass; classy desserts such as pitch-perfect crème brûlée. The cooking is spot-on, satisfying and pleasing and creative, but service needs to get up to speed to do the food justice. In a year or so, however, we reckon Mr Mills and Ferndale has what it takes to be one of the icon places to both eat and stay in Ireland. Keep an eye on this guy.

● **OPEN:** 7pm-9.30pm Wed-Sat; noon-2.30pm Sun
● **PRICE:** Dinner £27 (2 courses), £33 (3 courses), £38 (tasting menu). Lunch £16.50-£20.95
● **CREDIT CARDS:** Visa, Mastercard

● **NOTES:**
♿ access. Accommodation available, six en suite rooms.

● **DIRECTIONS:**
Coming from Enniskillen, cross the Cherrymount roundabout, then travel 1km on the Irvinestown road. Ferndale is on your right.

FONTANA

Colleen Bennett & Stephen McAuley
61a High Street, Holywood
County Down
℅ **028-9080 9908**
🖷 **028-9080 9901**
🖰 **www.fontanarestaurant.com**

Colleen Bennett's Fontana is on a mighty roll right now, serving supersonic food to delighted punters.

Fontana is one of those restaurants that seems to get better and better, by steady, accumulative, aggregate steps. Right now, the kitchen in Colleen Bennet's restaurant is firing out some mighty food, and it is served to happy punters in a sweet dining room by really excellent staff who look after you extra well. Oh, and they offer great value, and super wines. Could you want for more? No, you couldn't. Ms Bennet has always made a rip-roaring risotto and the current offering of prawn risotto with sweetcorn, courgettes, peas, chilli and coriander is one of the most subtle things you can eat, the flavours lifted by a suggestion of coconut. Superb potato and truffle oil soup; fab Drumgooland smoked salmon with blue Roosevelt potatoes, green beans, olives and egg; really fine grilled rainbow trout, and a knockout chocolate mousse with fresh raspberries that the McKenna children ate so swiftly that there wasn't a morsel left for the grown-ups to try.

● **OPEN:** noon-2.30pm, 5pm-9.30pm Tue-Fri; 6.30pm-10pm Sat; 11am-3pm Sun brunch
● **PRICE:** Lunch £15-£20, Dinner £25-£30
● **CREDIT CARDS:** Visa, Mastercard, Delta/Switch

● **NOTES:**
No ♿ access, but staff happy to assist up the stairs. Disabled toilet upstairs.

● **DIRECTIONS:**
On the main street in Holywood, in an alleyway, right between the opticians and the interiors shop.

GINGER

Simon McCance
68-72 Great Victoria Street
Belfast
County Antrim
℅ **048-9024 4421**
🖰 **www.ginger.ie**

Simon McCance is one of
the stars of Belfast city, with
a wholly original cooking
style that is all his own.

Simon McCance's cooking is like no one else's. His style is so original and so deft that he quickly made his name in a tiny room on the Ormeau Road, but the new city centre room means more folk can enjoy this singular and unique food. The best way to describe it is to say that McCance cooks the way he is: easy-going yet somewhat anxious; focused but not quite certain; unself-conscious and transparent. Other cooks seem to put technique between you and the ingredients: McCance just makes them sing all on their own: fried spiced squid is a dish everyone does, but his tastes different from anyone else's. Tempura of hake with a baby potato, green bean and ginger curry isn't a curry the way anyone else would do it, and who else would mix tempura with curry and make it such a riot of flavours? Soft centre chocolate cake is light and complete. There is asceticism in this man's culinary aesthetic, and it makes for some of the best eating to be had in contemporary Ireland.

● **OPEN:** noon-3pm Thu-Fri; 5pm-10pm Tue-Sat
● **PRICE:** Lunch €13.50 for 2 courses, €17.50 for 3 courses. Dinner €28.50
● **CREDIT CARDS:** Visa, Mastercard

● **NOTES:**
♿ access.

● **DIRECTIONS:**
200m up the street from the Crown Bar, leading out of the city and smack on the main strip of Great Victoria Street.

JAMES STREET SOUTH

Niall McKenna
21 James Street South
Belfast, County Antrim
✆ **028-9043 4310**
🖷 **028-9043 4310**
🖑 **www.jamesstreetsouth.co.uk**

Niall McKenna's pretty converted warehouse in the city centre is the Big-Night-Out destination in Belfast.

Niall McKenna's ultra-stylish restaurant is the epitomisation of the new Belfast Cool School.
The bland exterior on a narrow alleyway conceals JSS's wowee! dining room, and the staff are just as cool as the classy, elegant, understated style. Mr McKenna's cooking, then is clean, precise and classy: Lough Neagh eel with capers, tomato and crisp salad leaves with a balsamic dressing is a study in miniatures and textures, a dish as subtle as can be; a pitch-perfect and painterly artichoke and tomato risotto is mesmerisingly beautiful, so much so you pause before putting a fork to it; a sublime lemon posset with berries and chantilly cream is nursery food for grown-up food lovers. The food looks every bit as good as it tastes, and it works because it isn't in any way fashionable; this style of cooking is beyond fashion, and has its own aesthetic. The punters in JSS behave like a bunch of people who know when they are on to a good thing, and that good thing is the New Cool.

● **OPEN:** noon-2.45pm, 5.45pm-10.45pm Mon-Sat; 5.30pm-9pm Sun
● **PRICE:** Lunch £15.50, Dinner £25
● **CREDIT CARDS:** Visa, Mastercard, Amex, Switch

● **NOTES:**
♿ access. Pre-theatre menu £15.50 for 2 courses, £17.50 for 3 courses.

● **DIRECTIONS:**
From the City Hall, travel up Bedford Street, and James Street South is the first street on the right.

MACAU

Frankie Ho
271 Ormeau Road
Belfast
County Antrim
© **028-9069 1800**

Macau is a blast, thanks to Su Ling and her smart crew, and some punchy, friendly Chinese cooking.

Macau is the most fun to be had in Belfast. A tiny room halfway up the Ormeau Road is home to the best staff and the best buzz in the city and sitting here on any evening, you are confronted by a simple fact: people, people who have managed to get a table in Macau, are the luckiest people in the world. And they know it.

So, what's to love? For the McKenna children, bring on the chicken and sweetcorn soup, the chicken chow mein; the noodles with beansprouts and the beef with black beans and green peppers (OK, so give the green peppers to the old folks). For the McKenna parents, bring on the pork back ribs, the hot and sour soup, the monkfish and char siu hotpot, and the kai lan with ginger sauce. Fantastic service from Su-Ling and her team of shirt-and-tie waiters, a roaring buzz, and a tiny bill to which you add a big tip. Thumbs up to Frankie in the kitchen, and book a table as you leave, if you want to be one of the luckiest people in the world sometime soon.

- **OPEN:** 5.30pm-11pm Tue-Sun
- **PRICE:** Dinner £8-£12 per main course
- **CREDIT CARDS:** No credit cards

- **NOTES:**
♿ access.
Bring your own wine.

- **DIRECTIONS:**
From the city centre, go over the Ormeau bridge and the restaurant is in the little row of shops opposite the Ormeau Park.

NICK'S WAREHOUSE

Nick & Kathy Price
35-39 Hill Street
Belfast, County Antrim
✆ **028-9043 9690**
🖨 **028-9023 0514**
🖰 **www.nickswarehouse.co.uk**

Nick and Kathy Price are consummate restaurateurs, smart people who breathe the zeitgeist of Irish food.

Nick and Kathy Price have never stopped learning, have never stopped innovating, in all the years that they have been running cutting-edge establishments in Northern Ireland. This hunger for the new, along with a very primal vision of what constitutes good food – The Prices are members of and supporters of Slow Food, for example – graces their work with enormous cultural significance.
But that significance derives, first and foremost, from an appreciation of, and respect for, the pleasures of great food and great wines. So let's have some piquant salad with rare roast duck, or a simple plate of grilled sardines. let's have rare-breed pork, or perhaps fillet of salmon with sticky coconut rice. And if we want the funky and informal we will find it in The Anix, and if we want to be more formal we can go to the restaurant upstairs. Nick's Warehouse, more than any other restaurant, not only gives you what you want; it gives you what you need. That is a mighty achievement, from two very mighty people.

● **OPEN:** noon-3pm (wine bar) Mon-Fri, noon-2.30pm (restaurant) Tue-Fri; 6pm-9pm Tue-Thur; 6pm-10pm Fri-Sat
● **PRICE:** Wine Bar lunch £12, Restaurant lunch £18-£25, Dinner £27
● **CREDIT CARDS:** Visa, Mastercard, Amex, Diners

● **NOTES:**
♿ access, apart from small step at entrance.

● **DIRECTIONS:**
At the back of St Anne's Cathedral.

ROSCOFF BRASSERIE

Paul & Jeanne Rankin
7-11 Linenhall Street
Belfast
County Antrim
☎ **028-9031 1150**
🖰 **www.rankingroup.co.uk**

Roscoff Brasserie is the
classic done in a classy way,
as Paul Rankin goes back to
his classic culinary roots.

Roscoff Brasserie is the yin of Paul and Jeanne Rankin's
pair of benchmark Belfast restaurants, with the other,
Cayenne, most assuredly being the yang. RB is restrained
and feminine, whereas Cayenne is active and masculine.
Rb is restrained and direct, Cayenne is abstract and post-
modern. It's a logical and fun dichotomy, whichever one
you choose, but if you do choose the yin, then what you
you will get in Roscoff Brasserie is a classically subtle
room in the brasserie style, with cooking that comes
straight out of the classical canon: precise carpaccio of
beef with celeriac remoulade and Roquefort dressing;
spot-on chicken and ham hock terrine; rich duck breast
with Puy lentils; voluptuous lobster thermidor; delicate
filigree tart de jour. What Paul Rankin has done in RB has
been to return to his Roux Brothers, (remember them?)
roots, and he has done it in a intellectually understanding
and historically respectful way, and delivered it with a
finesse that is wholly winning.

● **OPEN:** noon-2.30pm Mon-Fri; 6pm-10.15pm Mon-
Thur; 6pm-11.15pm Fri & Sat. Closed Sun
● **PRICE:** Lunch £25-£30, or set menu of £15.25 for 2
courses, £19.50 for 3 courses. Dinner £25-£30 or set
menu of £21.50 for 2 courses, £27 for 3 courses.
● **CREDIT CARDS:** All major cards accepted

● **NOTES:**
♿ access.

● **DIRECTIONS:**
At the back of the City Hall in central Belfast.

SHU

Alan Reid
253 Lisburn Road
Belfast
County Antrim
✆ **028-9038 1655**
🖱 **www.shu-restaurant.com**

Brain McCann's cooking is raising the bar in Belfast, for this cook is a star turn, producing exciting cooking.

Alan Reid has always run a slick operation in Shu, but with the arrival of Brian McCann in the kitchen, he has a destination restaurant that will raise the bar in Belfast. Mr McCann has had lots of starry experience, but he has more than that. He is passionate, he understands seasonality, he has common sense, he is brimming with confidence and enthusiasm, and his food blows you away with its delicious, elegant simplicity: herb salad with buffalo mozzarella, oven-dried cherry tomatoes, and salted almonds; Glenarm salmon with steamed potatoes, fennel and lobster sauce; rump of lamb with potato fondant, artichokes, rosemary and balsamic jus. Crisped, firm, bright hake comes on a fine home-made tagliatelle with nutty, fried courgette, bursts of oven-dried cherries and a citrus gremolata. Macerated strawberries, in their own liquor and with fresh strawberry ice cream make a fitting end to a meal made with notably delicious ingredients and with a dexterous, light hand.

● **OPEN:** noon-12.30pm, 6pm-10pm
Mon-Sat
● **PRICE:** Lunch – 2 courses for £16, 3 courses for £22, Dinner £33
● **CREDIT CARDS:** Visa, Mastercard, Amex

● **NOTES:**
No ♿ access.

● **DIRECTIONS:**
Straight up the Lisburn Road, across the road from Windsor Avenue.

Keep in touch with what's happening in Irish food